NEW LIGHT ON DELINQUENCY
AND ITS TREATMENT

RESULTS OF A RESEARCH CONDUCTED FOR THE INSTITUTE OF HUMAN RELATIONS YALE UNIVERSITY

BY

WILLIAM HEALY, M.D.

AND

AUGUSTA F. BRONNER, Ph.D.

JUDGE BAKER GUIDANCE CENTER, BOSTON

GREENWOOD PRESS, PUBLISHERS
WESTPORT, CONNECTICUT

Copyright © 1936 by Yale University Press

All rights reserved.
Reprinted with permission of Yale University Press

First Greenwood Reprinting 1969

Library of Congress Catalogue Card Number 79-90525

SBN 8371-2253-8

PRINTED IN UNITED STATES OF AMERICA

PREFACE

The opportunity which the Institute of Human Relations of Yale University offered us for gaining new light on delinquency—its fundamental causes and better treatment—met a ready response on our part. In spite of the many studies of delinquency already produced, it is certain that various aspects of the subject need much more illumination. In reporting the research conducted for the Institute we above all wish to make clear the fact that we have won for ourselves, and we hope for others, some clearer understandings upon which to base more effective procedures with the juvenile delinquent. With the widening of horizons some exceedingly practical issues have been forced into sharper focus.

We believe that our present findings and formulations have significant values for those who officially or otherwise deal with delinquents, for those who are engaged in programs of prevention, and indeed for all students of the problems which delinquency presents. It is, then, to a wide range of readers that we address ourselves in this book. This has not been altogether easy because, while desiring to avoid amassing facts and figures, we have conceived it necessary to outline our methodology and incorporate enough factual material to justify the conclusions and generalizations that we wish to emphasize as applicable in practice.

(Every-day workers with delinquents may be less interested in scientific method and detail. To them we especially recommend Chapters I, V to IX inclusive, XI and XIV in which are to be found new viewpoints and new principles concerning causation and treatment possibilities.)

Our acknowledgments properly begin with tribute to Dean Robert M. Hutchins, now president of the University of Chicago, and to Mr. Donald Slesinger who first envisaged for us the possible values of this research. To President

Angell and the executive committee of the Institute we owe our freedom in carrying on the work. The Institute and we ourselves are under deep obligation to the Children's Fund of Michigan, established by Senator Couzens, for the financing of our Detroit Clinic and to Mr. William J. Norton and the other officers of the Fund for the fine coöperative spirit with which we were received. The continued interest of Mr. Mark A. May, the director of the Institute at Yale, has been greatly appreciated by us. The Trustees of the Judge Baker Guidance Center in Boston encouraged this project from its initial stage and more latterly have generously provided for its completion.

It is impossible to mention all those in the juvenile courts of the three cities and the personnel of the social agencies and of the schools and the members of the medical profession who have assisted us. The part they played is somewhat indicated in the chapter that describes the research. Without this friendly aid we could have accomplished nothing.

Our clinical units were disbanded before the follow-up work was undertaken and long before the writing of this book. In spite of all that the members of our staff have contributed to the research, they are not responsible for any of the final deductions or generalizations. But their loyalty and their industry deserve special mention.

The psychiatrists in the New Haven and Boston units were Dr. Edwin Gildea for one year and Dr. S. Spafford Ackerly for two years. Dr. Louis A. Schwartz served three years continuously in the Detroit Clinic.

The psychiatric social workers were Miss Ruth M. Belcher in New Haven; first Miss Alice Loomis and then Mrs. Mary L. Cochran in Boston; in Detroit Miss Marguerite Silliman and Miss Bernice Blackman, with, in the last year, Miss Winifred Ayling. Two students from the Smith School of Social Work, Miss Bradsher and Miss Gossett, had their field training in the New Haven Clinic.

Preface

In New Haven part-time psychological service was successively rendered by Mrs. Kimmel, Miss White and Miss Snedden. In Boston the mental testing was done by the psychological staff of the Guidance Center. The Detroit Clinic had the full-time service for one year of Miss Carol Thomas as psychologist and Mrs. Catherine Giblette for two years.

The statistical compilations and the evaluations of much of the data of the case-records were the work of Dr. Myra E. Shimberg, assisted by volunteers, Miss Pauline de Friez and Miss Natalie Appleton of Boston.

For much assistance during and since the working-period of the unit there we have been deeply obligated to Mrs. Frances Roth of New Haven, and to Mr. John C. McCarthy and Dr. Norma Cutts for their help in obtaining the later records of the delinquents. In Boston the expert volunteer service of Miss Edna Spitz has been invaluable in following up cases.

Especially we acknowledge our debt to Mr. James D. Bronner for much time given in critical re-evaluation of our data and aid in the early preparation of the manuscript. Nor can we omit mention of the devoted interest in our work displayed by various clerical assistants, volunteer tutors, and others.

The only publications from this research so far have been "Rebellion and Its Relation to Delinquency and Neurosis in Sixty Adolescents" by Dr. Ackerly, and "Social-Situation Pictures in the Psychiatric Interview" by Dr. Schwartz— both appearing in the *American Journal of Orthopsychiatry*.

W. H.
A. F. B.

Spring 1936.

CONTENTS

	PAGE
Preface	v
I. New Orientations—The Significance of Delinquency	1
II. Introduction to the Research	14
III. The Families	25
IV. The Delinquents	36
V. Studies of Delinquents and Non-Delinquents in the Same Families—Comparison of Personalities	53
VI. Comparison of Delinquents and Controls in Relation to Favorable and Inimical Family Situations	78
VII. The Twins—Delinquents and Controls	92
VIII. Comparison of Emotional Experiences—Delinquents and Controls	121
IX. The Meaningfulness of Delinquency for the Individual—A New Orientation	132
X. The Treatment Program	141
XI. Outcomes and New Orientations for Treatment	158
XII. Outcomes Correlated with Treatment	173
XIII. Other Data Correlated with Outcomes	190
XIV. Practical Implications of the Research	200
Index	225

NEW LIGHT ON DELINQUENCY
AND ITS TREATMENT

CHAPTER I
NEW ORIENTATIONS
THE SIGNIFICANCE OF DELINQUENCY

FOR better attacks upon the problem of juvenile delinquency, that forerunner of adult crime, new points of view are obviously needed. Since the results of dealing with the offender are so frequently disappointing, it must be that the basic forces producing delinquency and the obstacles to treatment have not been sufficiently considered and made clear. And most solutions proposed, embodying, as they usually do, some one idea about cause or cure, are easily seen to be not based on established fact, often unconsciously biased, and mainly futile. When scientific methods of investigation seek to connect cause and effect, the complexities of causation and the common weakness of treatment methods in vogue are unavoidably brought to light.

It has gradually been borne in upon us that a better conception of the significance of delinquency as one form of human behavior is an essential offering vastly better vantage points for its control. This appears in great contradistinction to the attitudes of those who dwell only upon the negative or destructive aspects of delinquency, who see delinquency merely as wrong-doing, as behavior which injures society—and consequently are concerned with nothing more than utilizing some means to put a stop to this social injury.

Our present research, with its long continued treatment program for serious offenders, has centered on the family life of delinquents and a comparison of the delinquent with a non-delinquent child in the same family. Our collected material reflects the growing emphasis, largely taken over from psychiatry, which all workers in the social sciences have found themselves forced to place upon human relationships and upon the emotional issues involved therein. The findings have much interest in and of themselves, but their chief value lies in their contribution to practical formulations. It is in the spirit of our inquiry to regard it as highly fortunate that through it some new and valuable outlooks on delinquency have been derived. Indeed the culmination of our study is represented by these new orientations.

The first of these is a new orientation concerning the general significance of delinquency as a phenomenon. As a mode of behavior which is one part of the stream of life's activities, it must have as much meaning in the total order of happenings as socially acceptable forms of conduct. It must in some fashion be equally as purposive from the standpoint of the individual's needs and urges. Stated in terms of a general principle, the origins of delinquency in every case unquestionably represent the expression of desires and urges which are otherwise unsatisfied. For the onlooker, delinquency merely signifies misconduct; for the offender it is just as much a response to inner drives and outer stimuli as any other kind of conduct. The sequence of causes leading up to delinquency we deal with later in this chapter.

Second, from this understanding of the general background of causation we may best discover the nature of the special personal experiences and the reactions thereto which have activated the delinquency of the given delinquent. Realizing that delinquency has purposiveness the question arises: for the individual what is the specific meaningfulness of his delinquency? Analysis of our research material as presented in Chapters VI to IX demonstrates the possibility and practical value of a new orientation relating to such meaningfulness.

Third, from our experimental studies of treatment we undertake a reorientation with regard to treatment possibilities.

The Significance of Delinquency

Upon the personality of the delinquent much attention has been centered in the last few decades. Delinquents have been studied in order to determine their deviations, if any; their constitutional, physical, mental, and emotional peculiarities have been scrutinized. And it still remains, as will be seen in the present material, that the importance of these factors is not to be gainsaid. The serious consideration of the case begins with all available data about constitutional and acquired characteristics. By constitution we mean the equipment with which the individual is born; acquired peculiarities are the result of what has happened to the individual, notably the diseases, injuries, endocrine imbalance, or nutritional privations that may have affected the individual in any way, particularly the functioning of the central nervous system.

Then we also have to reckon with the phenomena of early established reactive tendencies. These are established as the result of response to stimuli in early life situations, particularly within the family circle. These stimuli originate almost entirely through human relationships, and how powerful they may be in creating behavior trends is demonstrated very clearly in our comparative studies of delinquents and non-delinquents.

Before turning to the detailed research findings and the application of these newer ways of looking at them it is important to consider our first orientation—consideration of the development of delinquency as a special form of behavior.

Delinquency is one small part of the total stream of the individual's life activities and in its significance represents, equally with other behavior, a response to inner or outer pressures. In common with all voluntary activities, it is one variety of self-expression.

The terms by which delinquency is designated—larceny, truancy, breaking and entering, and so on—are descriptions of behavior which do not in the least indicate what is ex-

Diagram Showing the Development of Delinquent Behavior

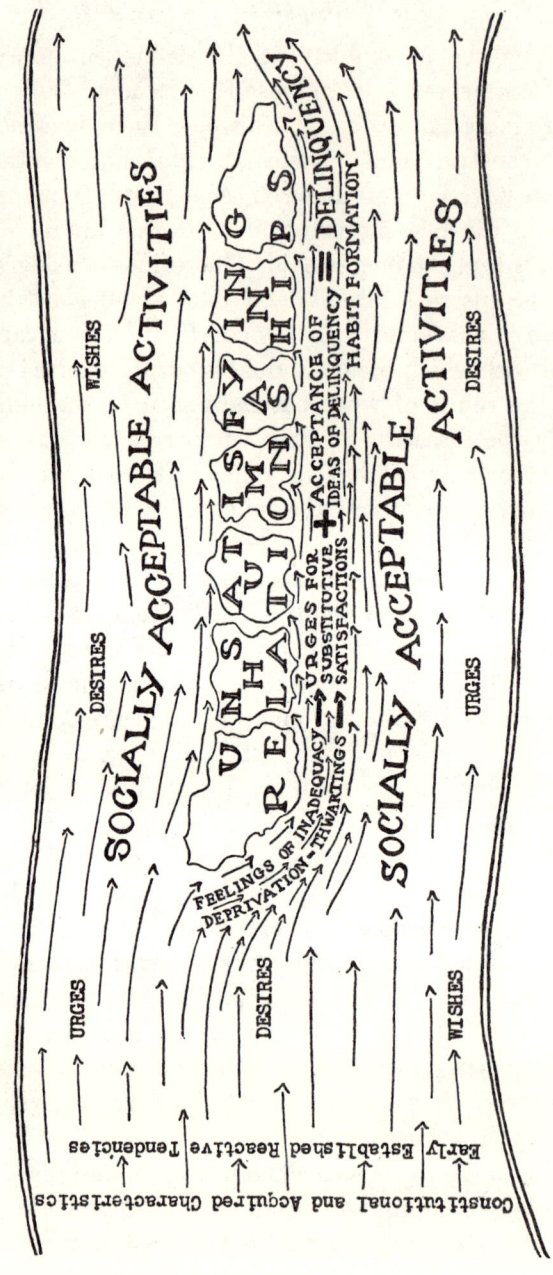

Unsatisfying human relationships form obstructions to the flow of normal urges, desires and wishes in the channels of socially acceptable activities. The deflected current of feelings of being inadequate, deprived or thwarted in ego or love satisfactions turns strongly into urges for substitutive satisfactions.

The obstructive relationships are mainly those within the family group where the attitudes and behavior of parents and others are influenced by their own personal dissatisfactions.

Underlying all these are current attitudes, beliefs, local and group ideologies—the ideas and practices of asocial individualism. These in turn are stimulated by social conditions and by easily observed exploitations, unfairnesses or dishonesties in business, law, politics, officialdom.

Ideas of delinquency are derived from companions, the observation of special temptations, reading, etc. These sources of ideas constitute environmental pressures. Through the acceptance of such ideas the deflected portion of the current of feelings and activities finds expression in delinquency.

pressed by the offender in the delinquent act. While it seems necessary to have labels for such types of conduct, yet it must be recognized in all common sense that naming the offense reveals nothing of the determinants of the behavior. It would seem equally obvious that it is just these determinants which must be known and coped with if effective treatment is to be undertaken.

Nor does it serve a better purpose to speak of delinquent, criminal, asocial, dissocial, or antisocial individuals. The prime matter for consideration is the fact that in only part of their activities are they delinquent or antisocial and that these particular behavior trends need explanation in terms of causation.

Contrast cases of the simple offense, truancy. One boy may be avoiding a situation in which he feels inadequate and discouraged; another has developed out of family life antagonism to all forms of authority—school representing one form; another has such need of recognition that, even though he does not dislike school, he truants in order to be "a regular fellow" with his companions; still another is the victim of peculiar anxieties which make the classroom hateful to him. However, in spite of the diversity of determinants, the authoritarian attitude toward all truancy and all truants is very likely to be the same, whether on the part of the school principal, the attendance officer, or the juvenile court.

This general principle applies to practically all offenses; the label of the offense gives little or no clue to its meaning as an activity which though swerved from the stream of socially acceptable behavior must originate in the desires, wishes, or urges that are fundamental in human nature.

The great driving forces which have strong emotional concomittants are the general fundamental desires for ego and affectional satisfactions. Specifically we must consider the desire for feeling secure in family and other social relationships, for feeling accepted by some person or group, for recognition as having some standing as a personality, for feeling adequate somehow or somewhere. The wish for various sorts of affectional response is allied to, though distinct from, desires for recognition, security, and adequacy. And there are other urges, such as those for accomplishment satisfying to oneself, for new experiences and adventures, for outlets for physical and mental energies, for ownership of possessions, for having, seeing, and doing. Normally with increasing age there is also the urge of self-assertion showing itself, for example, in desire for emancipation from childhood and family restrictions—the desire for independence and self-direction.

Interferences with these fundamental wishes are felt by the young person as thwartings and deprivations causing keen dissatisfactions. And since fundamental wishes as driving forces are integrated with the stream of active life, thwartings and deprivations tend to draw a part of the stream strongly into currents of activity which for the individual constitute substitutive satisfactions. Some activity must offset dissatisfactions, and delinquency offers one of the possibilities. Indeed a striking finding of our present study has been the immense amount of discoverable emotional discomfort that clearly has been part of the story of the origins of delinquency. On the other hand an acute contrast was brought out by the disclosure that very few indeed of the non-delinquents in the same families had in their emotional lives any such frustrations—and those few had found in channels other than delinquency some modes of compensatory satisfactions.

Now what form substitutive activities will take, whether or not they will be antisocial, depends partly on external circumstances, but mainly upon the acceptance of certain ideas. So far as ideas of delinquency are concerned, it is perfectly evident that in our stage of civilization these are derivable from many sources and that the potentiality of their virulent growth upon the fertile soil of youthful dissatisfactions is not to be denied. Of course it is the individual who has not primary or substitute satisfactions of other sorts who is prone to succumb to an impulse toward delinquency as the result of a combination of dissatisfactions and ideas about delinquency. The combination is found to show many varying aspects as either of the components differ. A boy, for example, feeling himself inadequate in other relationships finds himself accepted and gains recognition with a gang if he takes up with the suggestions they give him of stealing with or for them. Another may seize upon notions that he has gained from his reading and by entering into some hazardous solitary form of delinquency set out to prove merely to himself that he is not white-livered. An idea much dwelled on by many youngsters centers about the possible pleasures of independently making one's own way in the world—then, given a situation in which family discords make home life irksome, running away is the understandable result. The special temptations that the environment offers —the display of goods that can easily be stolen, the unlocked automobiles that are readily driven away, the observation of money that can be pilfered—make their impress upon the ideational life sometimes long before delinquency is entered upon.

But how does it happen that some young people living in the same family environment as the delinquent, with the desires common to youth, with the same social pressures, and always with ideas of delinquency easily obtainable, are able to refrain from antisocial conduct? We have often turned to consideration of the non-delinquent with the thought that it is more astonishing to discover that they have refrained from delinquency than that a brother or sister has developed antisocial behavior. It has been part of our task to study the personalities and lives of these non-delinquents for comparative purposes. In endeavoring to answer the question why ideas

The Significance of Delinquency

of delinquency have never been considered, or if considered why they have been rejected, we have had to take account of various differences in personality characteristics but in the main we have found the behavior derivatives of emotional satisfactions to be the answer. When there have been no intense feelings of deprivations, inadequacies, or thwartings as related to either ego-impulses or desires for affection, the individual has been able readily to find sufficient satisfactions in socially acceptable behavior. Our comparative studies of two children in the same family bring this out clearly and especially our studies of twins, one of whom was delinquent and one not delinquent.

As cause and effect most closely linked to the deeper satisfactions and dissatisfactions of children are the behavior attitudes of those in contact with the children. This stands out very plainly as we have compared the emotional lives of the delinquents with a brother or sister who has avoided delinquency. Many of the families from which the delinquents came lived in situations that could be considered thoroughly inimical for the upbringing of a child, yet even under these conditions it was clear that the non-delinquents had distinctly more satisfactory human relationships than had the delinquents.

It would be easy to generalize that parents through their own dissatisfactions arising from discrepancies between cultural or economic desires and the realities of their life situations could reasonably be expected to display asocial attitudes, even as exhibited in their behavior toward their children. But for our research it was most enlightening to uncover the additional fact that there had been great differences in their feelings and behavior toward their different children—more sympathetic understanding, more fulfillment of fundamental needs, less inconsistent treatment very frequently indeed having been exhibited from early years toward one child as compared to another.

As investigators of the stream of life's activities we are led to wonder why at various points there have not been dams or barriers which might have prevented the current from flowing in the direction of delinquency. We can readily understand that when a channel has been formed by habits of thought or by established social contacts the difficulties of checking the flow of activities are great. How often we have heard, "I got in the habit of stealing," or, "I couldn't stop going with those fellows!" Some more introspective youngsters have related to us their story of how thoughts, once started in this direction, returned again and again in idle or half-waking moments to ideas of delinquency—they had nothing else to absorb their interest, nothing else that gave them commanding satisfactions.

But aside from this matter of the strength of habit formation there remains the question why the delinquent early or later did not find in himself inhibiting forces strong enough to check delinquent impulses. As we looked into the lives of these young people, it was clear, for one thing, that social restraints and inhibitions were in many instances absent because of poor formation of what is so aptly termed an ego-ideal. There had been no strong emotional tie-up to anyone who presented a pattern of satisfactory social behavior. To put it in another way, the child had never had an affectional identification with one who seemed to him a good parent. The father or mother either had not played a rôle that was admired by the child or else on account of the lack of a deep love relationship was not accepted as an ideal.

We have found it impossible to present the above fact statistically for our series of cases, because it would have required a tremendous amount of time to analyze the emotional lives of the delinquents in order to gain subjective evidence that ego-ideals had not been an influence in their personality development; but the objective facts are plain enough. If from nowhere else, it would have been made clear to us from our present comparative studies that the effectiveness of moral teaching and of good example is dependent on emotional values attached to them by the child. The feeling tone about right conduct derives most powerfully from the emotional side of human relationships. Ethical concepts that have no personification have little force in the lives of young people.

But in contrast, when studying the non-delinquents we came across many striking evidences of influential ties to some person, nearly always a parent—sometimes an unworthy parent though not felt as such by the child—whose esteem was desired and was obtained and retained if the child remained non-delinquent. The importance of building up standards through such personal relationships can hardly be overstated.

We might go a step further in inquiring why the young individual finds in himself no barriers preventing his ideas and activities from flowing in channels of delinquent conduct. In particular we may ask, why has the delinquent in and of himself, arising from his own sense of what is right and wrong, no strong feeling about the wrongfulness of delinquency? Now it is very true that we constantly find the delinquent fully able to express his conscious belief that delinquency represents wrong conduct, but evidently his *feeling* about its wrongfulness has not been sufficiently strong to function as a preventive. How then does it happen, that the delinquent's personality is possessed of such an impotent categorical imperative, conscience, or superego? Why, for example, has "Thou shalt not steal" no strong sanctions for him?

To be sure, we have partly covered this point in the preceding discussion. We know that the introjection, as the analysts phrase it, of parental prohibitions, the absorption of parental ideas of right and wrong, is the anchorage of conscience long before the principles of good conduct are taught by church or school. Through the earliest prohibitions, even with regard to bodily functions, family possessions, or behavior in the family circle, the child develops a conscience or superego long before it comes to any question of social behavior outside the family. This is obvious, but it leaves the whole matter of the growth of the sense of right and wrong an extremely complicated problem.

The fact seems to be clear that the barrier which we call conscience or the superego is universally found, but in different individuals plays various and partial rôles in determining or motivating behavior. Hence conscience may cover only certain areas in the field of conduct. In one case of our series a young boy evidently had a strong conscience about being mannerly and doing his school work well, while stealing seemed really to mean nothing to him except as he might be caught for it. And we have noted in some instances that lying was quite condoned by conscience while stealing was a sin, and that in other cases this was exactly reversed.

A final consideration in this discussion of the development of delinquency as one special manifestation of behavior is the origins of the attitudes and beliefs of parents—just because these have so much to do with the development of conduct trends in their children. Quite apart from the knowledge we gained of the parents' scale of values resulting, more or less unconsciously, from the influences of their own early lives, there is another matter of vast import to general social welfare. Though we made no special study of this, it often cropped out that certain undesirable attitudes and behavior tendencies exhibited by parents were related, sometimes vaguely and sometimes explicitly, to prevalent asocial ideologies. Our population in general is well acquainted with the exploitations, unfairnesses, and dishonesties which are current in many spheres of activity. From this it follows that parents who feel deprivations and discomforts and who have not ideals that prevent can readily rationalize the situation. They may easily persuade themselves that, such being the state of things, the sensible behavior is to get what one can by whatever means are available, to consider one's own personal advantage at the expense of anything else, to enjoy oneself as best one can. It goes without saying that these sentiments based on current ideologies of self-considering individualism militate against the proper upbringing of children and specifically tend to pervade the household, spreading—though, for various reasons, differentially—from parents to members of the younger generation.

CHAPTER II

INTRODUCTION TO THE RESEARCH

THIS research incorporates certain distinctive features. The family, rather than the delinquent child alone, was regarded as the unit to be studied and dealt with. The treatment approach was integrated and controlled by scientific considerations of the various aspects of complex causations. To insure a broad outlook upon causations and upon the possibilities and blockings of treatment, the research was conducted simultaneously in three representative American cities. Then, an unique and certainly a most interesting feature of the work was the paired study of a delinquent and a non-delinquent sibling.[1]

This was the first project initiated under the Institute of Human Relations of Yale University. The formulation of it followed on the heels of the Detroit Conference in 1928 on "Family Life." At that time it was generally agreed that the next experimental step in the treatment of the offender should be through assailing causes originating in the home. From the bench, the pulpit, the school, and the social worker had come such accusations of the responsibility of the family for delinquency that it was held to be a matter of prime urgency to undertake studies of the extent to which family situations could be modified as they might be found to bear upon the production of delinquency. With so many contributing factors arising out of family life in which the child is still a dependent, it seems grossly illogical as well as unfair that the child, even though not considered solely blamable, is the sole recipient of treatment.

Originally a ten-year project was considered; later it

1. Throughout this book the current scientific term "sibling" will be used to denote a brother or sister.

Introduction to the Research

seemed better first to discover what five years of effort would show before planning any continuance of the program. But, through the economic exigencies which developed, unfortunately even this period had to be much shortened. This curtailment of the program left little opportunity for the establishment from time to time of newly directed efforts, such as were believed desirable and even necessary in order that critical evaluations of accomplishment might pave the way for improved methods of work. Knowledge of the possibilities of essentially altering situations and conditions that form background factors upon which delinquent tendencies develop is only to be acquired through long observation.

It has been possible, nevertheless, to garner from this incompleted project many interesting findings and to formulate some extremely valuable conclusions and new fundamental orientations which should be of great service in constructing further programs for the prevention of delinquency. These conclusions and newer points of view are based upon thoroughgoing analyses of the voluminous data gathered by the clinical units and upon assiduous attempts to follow the lives of the young offenders, obtaining facts from those who have had contact with them during the period since the work of the units ceased. This period of follow-up has been, of course, absolutely necessary in order to ascertain the effectiveness or failure of the treatment attempted.

If we suggest that the curtailment of the original program enforced too short a period for contemplated scientific re-attacks upon the diverse factors making for delinquency, we perhaps should also state that these three years of intensive study of delinquents and of attempts at treatment were at the close of nearly twenty-five years of experience in this field. The first scientific approach to the study of delinquents was begun in connection with the Chicago Juvenile Court in 1909. During the intervening years the directors of this research have, as part of their professional duties, continued to make etiological studies and to give diagnostic service concerning delinquents to courts and social agencies. Ample proof has been accumulated that the personality of the individual delinquent and the particulars of his life situation have to be taken into consideration for effective treatment. But an unfortunate and unscientific gap existed between the work of the diagnostician and of those who were attempting to modify the offender's conduct trends. It is only within the last few years that guidance clinics have made any attempt to control treatment.

This particular research was undertaken as an attempt to clear the way for laying down paths for treatment efforts —by learning what methods can best be employed, what resources are available, what blockings exist that can or cannot be met. The excursions into the field of treatment, whether resulting in failure or success, represent the applications of scientific methods. It is only by the development of scientific outlooks and appraisals in this as in most other fields of human endeavor that progress can be made.

The ample case-study records of this research have been carefully compiled and they contain much information that could never have been obtained unless confidential relationships had been professionally established. It is through this latter fact that it has been possible to delve much deeper into the underlying dynamic causations of delinquency than more superficial studies would have permitted.

At the outset there was agreement upon the point that the study should be conducted intensively with a small number of cases and families during a period of years. The therapeutic endeavor was to reach out into the offender's family circle, and to include anyone who seemed to be involved from an etiological standpoint in the problem of the delinquent.

The central point of each separate case-study, naturally, is one delinquent individual. The plan mainly adhered to

Introduction to the Research 17

was to *select for study only those recognizable as potentially serious offenders, those who had been repeatedly delinquent.* But for common-sense reasons certain other restrictions were placed upon the intake. No greater proportion of girls was to be accepted than the ordinary ratio of juvenile court cases shows—not more than one girl to three boys. The definitely feeble-minded were to be ruled out. All of the children and at least 75 per cent of the parents were to be able to speak English. Except for such limitations, the cases were to be unselected; they were to be taken from the courts as the case load permitted. None were to be ruled out because the coöperation of child or parent seemed difficult to win.

Certain other elements of selection did creep in to a limited extent because of the need for taking families where there was a comparable non-delinquent sibling. Some preference was given to cases where the delinquent was one of twins. The research was not undertaken with the purpose of accumulating statistics concerning delinquency, and we insist that our findings have no large statistical values—previous publications have sufficiently covered the ground.

There is very little doubt that, aside from the purposive omission of mental defectives, the cases taken are representative of the potentially serious offenders that appear before a juvenile court in American urban communities. Surveying the cases which the Detroit unit was asked to take, we have thought that perhaps a large proportion of exceptionally difficult delinquents were referred to us there; though this is possible, we have no proof of it. On the whole we must conclude that we have a fair sampling of the repeatedly delinquent, of the families from which such delinquents spring, and of the conditioning factors which make for delinquency.

The clinical units had quarters apart from the juvenile courts. In each city the staff consisted of a psychiatrist, a psychologist, and one or more social workers. The methods of study were the usual ones of the child guidance clinic.

Very careful psychological testing was undertaken not only for the purpose of ascertaining intelligence levels, but also for the sake of knowing educational qualifications and special capacities or disabilities. Physical examinations were made with attention to anthropometric details. If there were any indications of special abnormalities, the case was referred to medical clinics and hospitals where special investigations and physical treatment could be carried out. This was done in a great many cases; for example, some had the benefit of elaborate biochemical studies. The amount of psychiatric work done with the delinquent varied greatly according to the needs of the individual and the exigencies of the situation. Many were seen by the psychiatrist very repeatedly to discover the nature of their conflicts and dissatisfactions and in the attempt to resolve these troubles. The psychiatrist also sometimes had treatment interviews with parents and other relatives, but the main work with families was done by psychiatric social workers. Not infrequently relatives willingly came again and again to the office for therapeutic help; in other instances the social workers had to make many visits to the home. A vast number of contacts were made with schools, recreational centers, settlement houses, and other social agencies. Not only were the delinquents and relatives given personal help through interviews but various improvements of their life situations were attempted. They were helped through medical attention obtained for them; sometimes financial aid or employment was secured, or family budgeting was planned; new school adjustments were arranged and even special tutors supplied; some children were sent to summer camps, some were placed in foster homes. Above all, through the psychiatric type of service given, attention was paid whenever possible to emotional adjustments within the family circle. Something of the extent of service rendered and how much modification

Introduction to the Research

was found possible or successful appears later in the chapter on treatment.

In order to obtain a fair picture of what problems are presented by delinquents and what their typical situations are in American life, it was deemed advisable not to concentrate efforts in one community. Boston and New Haven were first chosen as research centers and then, through the fine cooperation of the Children's Fund of Michigan established by Senator Couzens, a research clinical unit was established in Detroit. The Boston and New Haven units began work in September 1929 and continued for approximately three years. The Detroit clinic which became active in September 1930 continued in operation until June 1933. With all the differences in the three cities the interest of the courts and of the social agencies in this research program proved unfailing. Within their limitations their resources were drawn upon by us and indeed without their admirable display of good will our treatment program would have availed little and the gathering of factual data for our conclusions would have been considerably limited.

Some comparisons of the social situations and of the organizations in the different cities and of the working conditions for the research units are necessary to fill out the picture.

The Boston Juvenile Court serves only part of the city; in comparison with other juvenile courts of large cities it consequently has fewer cases brought before it. It has no detention home; cases are heard very speedily after complaints are filed or arrests are made, nearly all delinquents in the meantime being allowed to go to their own homes. The judge, permanently appointed and serving full time, was cooperative but felt that, once the case was turned over to the research unit, treatment should proceed without any help whatever from the court. No funds in Boston are available from the court for placement of children or for any major plans of treatment; other sources must be tapped. Through the existence of many agencies for children in Boston the opportunities for securing desired help are rather favorable, especially as the coöperative spirit is admirable. An exception is the school department in Boston which, as a whole, compared with the school systems in the other cities takes very little interest in the problems of delinquency.

New Haven being a city of less population, the juvenile court naturally is a smaller organization. The bulk of the cases coming before the court are of Italian parentage, as would be expected where that nationality forms such a large proportion of the inhabitants. The court utilizes a small and pleasant detention home which, however, presents some of the difficulties which exist wherever delinquents are housed together, difficulties in wholesomely occupying the time of those detained and in preventing delinquent contagion. At the time of our research a school for truants operated in the same building and received the detained delinquents, an arrangement which we found could readily complicate the situation if the teacher took sides for or against the child or influenced his attitudes toward court or clinic. Two judges, the major portion of whose time was devoted to private practice and whose appointed terms were comparatively short, rotated in service. The probation officers were few and less well trained than in the other cities; we found that they often had already established unfortunate attitudes in delinquents and parents which were hard to break down. Our research unit found the court interested, but it had little to offer; we were, however, particularly aided by the assistant district attorney in charge of domestic relations. New Haven had comparatively few social agencies with resources for children, particularly for placement or foster homes. The school department, on the other hand, especially through its administrative heads, was keenly alive to the problem of delinquency and was found extremely helpful in carrying out treatment plans relating to education. Aside from what the schools could offer, we found many limitations in treatment possibilities in New Haven.

The clinics in Boston and New Haven divided the services of a psychiatrist, but in Boston there were always others from the staff of the Judge Baker Guidance Center who could be called upon for assistance. In both places the psychological work was amply provided for; and each unit had a psychiatric social worker.

In Detroit with its greatly varied population the situation was quite different. The court there is a very large organization, giving service to the entire city, operating in a building attached to the recently constructed detention home in which considerable numbers of delinquents are held. Many were customarily detained for a month or more before disposition was made of their cases. The judges are elected for a period of six years. During the years of our research the court was served by a judge of long experience and training —as the clinic closed a political turnover removed him. Great interest was shown in the advent of the research unit and it was utilized partially for the training of probation officers. It was thought of as a demonstration clinic and, as stated above, often particularly difficult cases were referred to it. The court has funds for the placement of children so that there was a greater permanence of oversight and control of foster home cases. The community as a whole has many resources for recreation and special training and its social agencies are very active. The coöperation of the school officials was most excellent. Our clinic there was much more liberally supplied with funds than the other two units which were on the budget of the Institute of Human Relations. Its quarters were by far the most adequate, having an attractive playroom for children. From the Childrens Fund money was available for summer camp projects and for other purposes.

In the unit there was a full-time psychiatrist, one psychologist, and during the last year three full-time psychiatric social workers.

Obviously it is quite unfair to make comparisons of the outcomes of treatment attempted in the three units. Conditions and available resources varied greatly in the three cities and there were unavoidable differences in the nature of the cases taken. Our main conclusions are to be drawn as they are focused upon the possibilities of treatment with different types of delinquents and different types of family situations—all as related to the machinery which society has set up for handling delinquents, and to the reconstructive resources available in the community.

Some conception of the intensive nature of this research may be gained from a statement of the number of individuals involved in the study.

<pre>
                    133 FAMILIES STUDIED
              (574 members of families worked with)
              | |
145 Non-delinquents Studied   153 Delinquents Studied
              | |
              | 143 Delinquents Accepted
              | For Treatment
              | |
              | ----------------------
           Utilized as   Delinquents Paired   Delinquents Without
           Controls   With Controls   Controls
              105   105   38
</pre>

The very essence of this research lies in the fact that no theoretical paths have been pursued as related either to causations or treatment. With the opportunity for deeper studies of factual material than have been hitherto possible, the main aim always was to discover the forces creating de-

Introduction to the Research

linquent trends which were actively at play within the individual or between him and his intimate environment. We naturally asked ourselves many questions: Is the problem mainly that of the delinquent himself—a problem of his own nature, or is it a problem arising from his own conditioning experiences? Are the great sources of delinquency really those of family life—parental attitudes, economic stresses, unfortunate patterns of family behavior? When family situations are at fault, is there much promise of their being modified? Do delinquents ever come from decently living, normally adjusted family groups? To what extent are the main causations of delinquency found outside of family life? What has been the effect of various forms of treatment instigated under the law? In becoming an offender, to what does the delinquent succumb, or is he expressing himself rather than succumbing? Is the main problem that of general social pathology, *e.g.*, delinquent group attitudes, external temptations, current ideologies, etc.? Under such general question headings many others were subsumed.

But no line of inquiry concerning causations seemed likely to be more fruitful than the key question: Why has a comparable sibling in the same family not been delinquent? Through comparison does the delinquent appear to be a deviate, or is he the more normal individual? Has he had different conditioning experiences; has he in any way stood in a special relationship to his parents? Has he been in contrasting situations outside the family life? Has he had a different health history?

The challenge of these common-sense questions which can only be answered by thoroughgoing scientific inquiry led to the attempt to make comparative studies of as many non-delinquents as possible. A sibling of the same sex if available and as near the same age as could be obtained was selected for study. We were finally able to accumulate adequate data for 105 pairs of delinquent and non-delinquent siblings, including 8 pairs of twins (the compared non-delinquents we designate "controls"). The interpretation of data concerning these pairs of cases forms, as naturally would be expected, one of the most significant portions of the research.

CHAPTER III

THE FAMILIES

THE knowledge which this research affords of situations in family life from whence delinquency arises and, more especially, discoveries of what is going on below the surface of ordinarily observable family conditions offers vastly stimulating material for reflection concerning the real origins of delinquency and the building of criminal careers.

Without for the moment passing judgment on the extent to which family life is responsible for the development of delinquent trends in the child, nevertheless our first consideration is that the family, as the primary social unit, is the matrix of earliest and closest relationships from which the career emerges. If not the *fons et origo* of criminalistic behavior, yet family life in cases of delinquency has not proved to be the bulwark of defense against growth of antisocial behavior which in the formulated ideal of our civilization it is supposed to be. The phrase "bringing up the child" connotes, above all, the shaping of behavior patterns by the family.

Of course we acknowledge from the start that extraneous to family life there are many features of the American scene, often unfortunately deeply imbedded in it, which tend to make delinquency flourish among us. It is on account of this that comparisons of the amount and the kinds of delinquency and crime as they exist in other countries and here are in large measure valueless for planning our own betterment in terms of official procedures which seem to have been successful elsewhere.

But since fundamental drives and urges are common to all mankind the deeper origins of antisocial behavior must everywhere be the same. The summing-up of causes, **if we would really understand why delinquency or crime is a mode of human behavior, must include the general underlying motives of conduct as we have given them in our first orientation.** But the specific reactions of the individual, as our research evidences, are primarily due to influences arising from formative experiences or conditionings in early family life; only secondarily are the specific reactions to be thought of as caused by later extra-familial social pressures.

Before making any other interpretations which our collected material may warrant, the nature of our inquiry into the family life of delinquents and certain data about the groups dealt with should be presented.

Since one of the main purposes of the study was determination of the part that family life plays in the genesis of delinquency, a pertinent question is: Does long acquaintance with families during which effort is made to establish friendly, confidential, and helpful relationships, throw any new light upon the dynamic backgrounds which tend to produce delinquency? Our accumulated material answers this with a strong affirmative.

Studies which have heretofore been made by ourselves and others have necessarily been confined to the more readily obtainable surface facts. Though such data have some interest and significance, it becomes clear through the intimate knowledge of families gained in this research that the less tangible facts, namely, those related to emotional attitudes and to values held, have greatest bearing on the problem.

But largely in order to show that the population we worked with was representative, constituting a fair sample of the cases which come to the juvenile courts in the three cities, we give for our 133 families (who had produced 194 delinquent children among 461 old enough to be delinquent) the routine data which are ordinarily gathered concerning

The Families

the families of delinquents. However, it must be recognized that, on account of the multitude of differences which exist, no adequate picture of the family backgrounds of delinquents can be sketched through stating averages and percentages. And always it must be remembered that we are dealing only with delinquents who happen to come before the juvenile courts. The child guidance clinics, seeing problem cases for families, social agencies, and schools, know that selective principles are at work that determine which delinquent appears in the juvenile court.

The figures given at the end of this chapter for nationality, religion, number of children, broken homes, step-parents, and illegitimacy in our groups show no great variation from the many statistical reports concerning the families of delinquents in these and other communities. The economic conditions of our families naturally reflect the period of depression and unemployment during which this study was made. Only about a third of the families were enjoying an adequate income, about half existed on marginal resources, 16 per cent were dependent on public aid at the time of our study. As might be expected, in many cases there was crowded housing and the neighborhood conditions were to be rated as distinctly poor.

To avoid tiresome statistical details and at the same time to attempt an enumeration of facts which may approximate a characterization of the parents, it is worth while to list some obvious deviations from figures for the general population. (Here again it must be noted that in the selection of cases the attempt was made to avoid studying mentally defective delinquents.) In doing this we can offer some roughly accurate estimations of the personality attributes of the parents in our 133 families. In most cases they were quite well enough known for this purpose by two or more members of the staff.

	Percentages
Both parents little or no education	36
Both parents dull or subnormal mentally	10
Both parents average or above in intelligence	50
Parent had court record (definitely criminal or notoriously immoral 12%, minor offenses 8%)	20
Parent heavily alcoholic—more than rarely intoxicated; in all but 2 cases the father	26
Father's interests (aside from alcoholism) poor or vicious	13
Father's interests good	24
Mother worked after marriage	49

	Father	Mother
	Percentages	
Superior personality qualities	6	11
No outstanding personality liabilities	46	52
Outstanding personality liabilities	36	32
High ethical standards	8	5
Poor ethical standards	21	15
Poor emotional control	28	30
Abnormal personality, neurotic or psychotic	10	11
Satisfactory social relations outside the home and place of work	12	13

This table of facts makes it clear that in very many of our families the opportunities ordinarily regarded as necessary for absorption of good ideals from parental example or for the development of respectful attitudes toward parental personality and authority were decidedly lacking. Yet, as we show in our chapter on the comparison of delinquents and non-delinquents in the same family, such data may or may not have bearing on the genesis of delinquency. Statistics of surface facts do not tell the real story.

To discuss each of these items would lead only to platitudes, and combinations of them with their overlappings would bring forth only more figures. However from the data recorded in great detail about these families it has been possible to make a synthetic picture of the conditions in each

The Families 29

case. A specially critical study was made of the assets and liabilities of family life in terms of:

A. Reasonably good home conditions from the standpoint of stability, living conditions, normal recreational opportunities.

B. Reasonably good family attitudes from the standpoint of avoidance of friction, rational treatment of children, and being law-abiding.

C. Neighborhood not distinctly bad from the standpoint of inimical influences.

For the entire 153 delinquents with whom we began to work we found that in only 22 instances did they live under conditions that for all of the above three categories were reasonably favorable, and in only 19 more were there two of the good conditions present. And it should be noted that in framing this classification of fundamentally decent life situations we have merely tried to keep within the bounds of moderate expectation of what seems requisite for the growth of children in right patterns of behavior.

It was rather remarkable to find that in only one of the 22 families who were preserving conditions not apparently inimical was there more than one delinquent. Partial explanation of the occurrence of any delinquents in these comparatively satisfactory homes lies in the fact that there were 9 instances of markedly neurotic or otherwise abnormal personality and 5 cases of severe adolescent upset among the 23 offenders. The other 111 families showed a marked contrast: 45 of them had more than one delinquent child although their children of delinquent age—seven years and older—averaged somewhat fewer in number. This ratio of 1:22 as against 45:111 (or 9:22) tends to prove strongly that whatever else there may be that serves to prevent some children from becoming delinquent, the family environment, even if we do not include the subtler emotional interrelationships that we dwell on in later chapters, does play a rôle in the production of antisocial conduct.

Through the continuing friendly relationship between the professional staff of social workers and psychiatrist and the parents, much was learned of the facts and causes of established family attitudes. Sometimes knowledge of a personality was slowly built up, bit by bit, as factual items were recorded, and, at the opposite extreme, sometimes volumes of outpourings concerning parental lives early assailed the listener's ears. Altogether much was accumulated that bore not only on the cause of material conditions of home life but also upon exhibition in the family circle of attitudes and beliefs and feeling tones. All this naturally had been reflected in the life experiences of the children. Any account of it almost defies summation, and we are far from convinced that parents' verbalizations about their own lives were always correct, but it is probably nearly accurate to state that there was real disharmony between the parents in 54 per cent and distinct harmony in only 30 per cent. This, of course, means that in a large share of the families there was between the parents open exhibition of disrespect, discontent, and friction, with disagreement (in 41 per cent) about discipline of the children, especially of the delinquent. Sexual incompatibility was freely spoken of in 63 per cent of 75 families where parents discussed their sexual adjustments. (Only 15 per cent of parents in the series were separated or divorced.) The household was clearly dominated by the father in 44 and by the mother in 31 per cent. There was definite conflict between parents and children resulting from the clash between old and new world standards in one quarter of the families.

About the religious or church interests of these parents we have rather accurate information. In just half the families one or both parents had strong enough religious feelings to be at least regular church attendants. Included are 22 families in which one, if not both, of the parents are devoutly religious. In one third of the families there was irregular church attendance on the part of the parents. In the remaining 17 per cent neither parent was churchgoing.

Inasmuch as there were not only delinquents but also nondelinquent children in these families, it is very difficult to draw conclusions about the facts that are presented in the preceding two paragraphs. The attitudes of the child himself and his ideas and feelings as he lived in the family must be thoroughly taken into consideration if we attempt to evaluate the influence of any of these matters.

The attitudes of parents toward their delinquent children before we began our study of them could with fair approximation be established for 136 cases in 129 families—it being noteworthy that in many instances the attitudes of the father and mother were very different and that sometimes two delinquents in the same family were regarded and treated very differently.

Parents mainly unaware of problem	12 per cent
Both parents had refused to recognize problem as serious	32 per cent
At least one parent had attempted to understand problem but was unable to cope with it	34 per cent
Problem recognized and attempt to meet problem by much corporal punishment	22 per cent

Despite our knowledge that human attitudes are largely formed by early experiences, parents show such contrasting and varying reactions, even varying toward their different children, that the cause of their attitudes is not to be distinguished except by prolonged study of each case. One father may assert that since harsh discipline made a man of him, he intends to be severe with his children. Another says that he would rather treat his children too softly than make them suffer as he did. One quarter of the parents, about the same number of fathers and mothers, considered that their own early lives had been unhappy—frequently they complained that they had worked hard too early or had been too severely disciplined. Only a very small number consciously felt that they in their childhood love relationships had been rejected by their parents—or, on the contrary, had been "spoiled children." Though we have an account of only 10 per cent of the mothers in our series being overprotected or spoiled as children, the mothers themselves showed overprotection or spoiling with 34 per cent of the delinquents. And contrasting behavior, that of emotional rejection of the delinquent child, was exhibited by the fathers in 31 and the mothers in 37 per cent, whereas only 5 per cent of the parents considered that they had not been loved by their own parents.

In summation it seems clear that it is quite impossible to picture the family life in any single case from such statistical statements, even though for our series we have added many more items of deeper significance than are usually given in social studies and than we ourselves have presented in previous publications. Knowing from experience what counts most in the character development of children, we have here added to the more objective considerations of housing, neighborhood conditions, and economic status data for some of the less tangible qualities of family life, in order to depict in part, at least, the atmosphere and spirit that prevails in most of these homes. When all the handicaps are totaled, even allowing for the heaping up of inimical factors in single cases, it makes indeed a sorry picture, especially when compared with the requisites for wholesome upbringing—such as those, for example, set forth in the Children's Charter of the White House Conference on Child Life.

But surely since many children in these families have avoided delinquency we must have omitted some possible assets which are hidden in the backgrounds of family life. We shall later consider the causes of the differences in reactions of different children to apparently the same familial handicaps. How have these latter affected growing attitudes and beliefs? The evil influences of any item can only be established in terms of its meaningfulness for the individual child. One could give many illustrations of surprising and unexpected reactions—such as the concern of a shoplifting mother for the moral welfare of her children, the chaste sympathy of a girl for her immoral mother, the lesson which a lazy and dissolute father has meant to his boys.

And when either father or mother seems to be an outstandingly unfortunate influence, sometimes the other parent has appeared to have been much more potent in forming the character of a given child. Numerous instances could be given of this. As we shall see later, almost all of the presumably inimical factors in family life can be and sometimes are negligible for the development of character, if some one strong positive constructive relationship influences the growing child. On the other hand, some single destructive relationship may be enough to turn the tide of conduct tendencies in the wrong direction. The problem of explaining what has happened seems mainly to center in solving the equation, $a + x = y$, in which a represents the known environmental situation; x the established reactive tendencies of the child, partly established through constitutional characteristics but largely through prior emotional experiences in family life; and y the known conduct trends of the young individual.

Even though the conclusion must be reached that the negatively or positively bad influences in these families heavily outweigh the favorable, yet for any single case any of the supposed influences have to be evaluated as they may or may not have affected the child's conduct. If this were not so, how does it happen that such a considerable proportion of the children in these families do not become delinquent? The discussion of the active causes of the differences in behavior will be found in the chapters which deal with comparisons of delinquents and non-delinquent siblings.

GENERAL STATISTICS FOR THE 133 FAMILIES

	Percentage
Nationality of Parents	
United States	35
Italian	17
Polish	10
Foreign Jewish	3
Other nationalities	16
Marriages of mixed nationality	19
Religion	
Protestant	27
Roman Catholic	58
Jewish	4
Marriages of mixed religion	11
Occupational Status	
Father skilled worker	47
Father unskilled worker	40
Professional or "white collar" class	13
Work record	
Father steady worker	56
Father some unemployment	17
Father very irregular worker	27
Economic Status	
Comfortable income or better	33
Marginal income	51
Dependent on aid at time case seen	16
Home Conditions	
Unduly crowded	44
Poor hygiene	17
Good hygiene	50
Fair hygiene	33
Neighborhood Conditions	
Poor	37
Fair	38
Good	25

The Families

Social
- Deterioration — 17
- Helped by 5 or more social agencies — 38

Parental Status (for the delinquent)
- Both parents in the home — 65.5
- Both parents dead — 1.5
- Father dead — 10
- Mother dead — 6
- Parents separated or divorced — 15
- Delinquent child illegitimate — 5
- Step-parent — 12
- Foster or adoptive home — 6

CHAPTER IV

THE DELINQUENTS

WHAT manner of young person is the delinquent who has been studied in this research? This is a question that will naturally be asked, but to attempt any composite picture of these juvenile offenders, with all their diversified characteristics and attitudes, is to put ourselves in the unsound position of those who generalize so easily about "the criminal." On the other hand, to say that, except for the omission of the mentally defective, these young offenders represent the usual run of serious juvenile court cases and largely form the raw material out of which criminals are made will not be enough to satisfy the reader. So out of the hundreds of details that could be collected from our wealth of recorded material[1] we shall here with broad strokes sketch the makeup of the group, leaving many of the finer points for the important discussion of delinquents as compared with non-delinquents.

Our intensively studied series of cases is so small in number that no large statistical values are forthcoming to add to the data concerning delinquents in general. But our compilation of data on the more dynamic factors in these young lives gives greater enlightenment on the genesis of delinquency than we have heretofore possessed. However, again, these factors stand out most strongly when the two groups are contrasted.

1. Our figures for some of the items are not quite complete, but are roughly accurate enough to be accepted as adequately picturing the facts. There might have been some slight statistical differences if every item for every case had been obtainable. Adoptive parents, for example, or a father whose wife had died did not always know the full facts of the child's early life. In the main these figures are for 153 delinquents.

The Delinquents

General Data

THE usually gathered statistics for our series of the 153 delinquents first taken for study tell much the same story that has been told about juvenile court cases many times before. The proportion of boys to girls was about six to one—there were 130 boys and 23 girls. The modal age was between 12 and 14 years. The delinquent was the oldest or the youngest child of the family in 25 and 12 per cent respectively.[2] Seven of the delinquents were illegitimate children.

The first known delinquency occurred at eight years or earlier in 48 per cent and after twelve years in only 22 per cent. The delinquent had been delinquent for more than a year before his first court appearance in 87 per cent of the cases. These important facts obtained from more intensive studies than we have ever before undertaken demonstrate how early untoward forces must be at work which make for delinquency. And these findings are equally impressive in serving to show at what life period adequate measures for understanding and preventing delinquent tendencies should be undertaken.

The delinquents in court, though on serious complaints, were there for the first time in 40 per cent of the cases, but we found later that court appearance represented a first offense in merely 5 per cent. Recidivism, namely reappearance in court, had been exhibited to a varying extent, running as high as 11 times in court and, in some instances, an equal number of times in detention homes. The frequent ineffectiveness of punishment or of ordinary court or probation procedure is obvious.

2. We have shown in a previous study of three thousand unselected delinquents that in only 10 per cent of these was the delinquent an only child. So our selection of cases that had at least one sibling in order that we might study a non-delinquent in the same family does not by itself materially weaken our material as being representative of juvenile court delinquents. See *Delinquents and Criminals—Their Making and Unmaking*, New York, 1926.

The offenses committed were quite the usual ones listed on the complaint records of a juvenile court. Stealing, whether designated as pilfering, shoplifting, or larceny, was much the commonest. Next most frequent were such offenses as truancy, running away from home, and staying out all night. Then in order comes breaking and entering—36 per cent. Besides the latter, the fact that there were two cases of forging and one of manslaughter and that our studies revealed such earlier offenses as an attempted murder, two attempted suicides, and numerous thefts of automobiles for which the offenders were not in court shows that some of the more serious delinquencies were rather strongly represented in our group. So far as sex offenses are concerned, we learned, for the most part aside from the court record, of repeated homosexual and heterosexual experiences in 18 and 13 per cent respectively. So what we have long known is once more demonstrated, namely, that the establishment of confidential relationships brings to light vastly more delinquency than the offender is charged with in the juvenile court.

Heredity

Though we know how inaccurate the popular concept of heredity is as related to the origins of delinquency, an account of our findings that some might consider to have bearing upon the heredity of the delinquents in our series seems called for. Perhaps alcoholism, psychosis, epilepsy, and criminalism as these appear in the forbears will be regarded as important and for these the figures as known for our 133 families run as follow:

| | Parents | Grandparents |
	Cases	
Heavily alcoholic	35	18
Psychosis	8	6
Epilepsy	1	2
Criminalism	16	6
Prostitution	2	..

We have covered this ground before in previous publications and see in our present material no reason to change our opinion that except where the basis for delinquency exists in mental abnormality there is no good proof of the inheritance of such behavior characteristics as delinquency and criminality.[3] In two of our cases, one an epileptic with a probable epileptic personality who has an epileptic father, and one whose assaultive delinquent behavior was maniacal in type and whose father is a manic-depressive the significance of the inheritance is clear. But it is interesting to note that this latter boy has a twin and seven other siblings all of whom appeared to be normal mentally.

The point may well be made that, as biological science advances, the knowledge of what is likely to be carried over to descendants in the human species seems to be less and less certain. Non-delinquents as well as delinquents in the same families give evidence that very differently behaving individuals may come from the same stock. The fact of the matter is that unless we really know what the chromosomes and genes carry over we can never be in the position to evaluate heredity. We may quote ourselves, "It appears hazardous to offer any conclusion concerning the possible relationship of heredity to delinquency. Among the difficulties of interpretation is the fact that there are so often, surrounding youth, bad social situations created by socially unfit parents, the effects of which are not those of biological inheritance."

Physical and Mental Data

TURNING now to the developmental experiences and physical equipment of these delinquents and giving merely some of the more outstanding facts, we may begin by stating that

3. See, for example, "Inheritance as a Factor in Criminality. A Study of a Thousand Cases of Young Repeated Offenders," by Edith R. Spaulding and William Healy, *Bulletin of the American Academy of Medicine*, February 1914; and *Delinquents and Criminals, Their Making and Unmaking*, New York, 1926.

for the most part the *health history* has usually very little direct meaning for us here. It is only when comparisons are made with data obtained through similar inquiries about non-delinquents that any possible bearing upon the genesis of delinquency is shown.

An obvious exception is found in the cases of damage to the brain. A reliable account of severe *head injury* was obtained in 9 instances—clearly a much greater proportion than for the general population. These findings fall in line with our figures for larger series of delinquents. And we should state that our judgment on the severity of the injury was based on hospital reports or histories of a considerable period of unconsciousness following the accident. While every case has to be interpreted for itself, in general the after effects of such injuries in producing behavior instabilities is well known.

Likewise the physical status of the delinquent at the time of the study could only be shown to have meaning for the production of delinquency in rare cases, and then usually very indirectly. For any given individual the meaning of the *physical deviations* given at the end of this chapter are not clear as related to the causation of conduct trends, except as they may be related to emotional and social life—producing inferiority situations and dissatisfactions, for instance. An interesting question, again, is how these findings in total compare to those of non-delinquents.

A number of the cases were considered to be possibly suffering from *endocrinopathy*. Very thorough biochemical studies were made of some and a considerable, but less complete study of others. In six instances the clear diagnosis of glandular dysfunction was made and four others were suspicious cases. In all of these some relationship of their physical trouble to their delinquency was evident, but, of course, very indirect. The causations in every case are complex, and

The Delinquents 41

it must be remembered that very many individuals with the same physical malfunctioning do not become delinquent.

Marked *deformities or anomalies* of structural development were found in about 5 per cent of the cases we carefully studied for comparison with non-delinquents. Undoubtedly in these cases inferiority situations and feelings of inferiority resulted. But once more we have to ask whether or not the non-delinquents were also likewise handicapped.

Except as showing the material with which we were working when the attempt at treatment was undertaken, our figures on the results of *psychological testing* of the whole series of 153 delinquents have little statistical value. The testing which was done by well-trained psychologists showed a curve of distribution closely similar to that for the general population—see Mental Test Findings at end of chapter. (Of course since we deliberately tried to avoid working with mental defectives our series in that particular is not entirely representative of juvenile court cases. However, in spite of our first judgment, two per cent of the delinquents proved to be high grade defectives.) After all, the main interest of the psychological findings lies in comparison of the delinquents with the non-delinquents.

It has been sometimes said that delinquents in general tend to show more ability for manual tasks and occupations, more ability to work with concrete material than they demonstrate for the more intellectual work that is demanded in tests used for intelligence rating. We did not find this substantiated by special tests given. Only about 25 per cent showed any such marked ability.

Though extreme school dissatisfaction was expressed by many delinquents we were surprised to find that careful psychological testing failed to reveal in this series any clear-cut cases of such special disability for school subjects as reading disability.

An exceedingly careful attempt was made to diagnose the delinquent, as we came to know him, in terms of normality versus *personality deviation*, and normality versus *neurosis* and *psychosis*. If scientific conservatism is the aim, this represents a difficult task, especially when estimating the mental status of emotionally disturbed children and adolescents. We took great pains and exercised much caution in making classifications. For the 153 cases with whom the study was begun we offer the following striking figures:

	Definite diagnosis	Probable diagnosis	Possible diagnosis
Neurosis or psychoneurosis	19	3	1
Mild or early psychosis	5	2	1
Abnormal personality			
Constitutional inferior personality	2	..	..
Egocentric unstable personality	2	..	..
Schizoid personality	1	..	..
Unclassified	1	..	..
Post traumatic personality	3	..	..
Post encephalitic personality	1	1	..
Epileptic personality	1	1	..
Homosexual personality	1	..	1
	36	7	3

The diagnosis in none of these cases was made on the basis of the delinquent manifestations alone. Even when these seemed grossly irrational in the sense of being frequently repeated although followed by many unpleasant consequences that would seem far to outweigh any possible temporary satisfactions that delinquency might offer, we did not regard the behavior as necessarily indicative of abnormality. For example, we did not include the boy of thirteen, normal physically and of quite good intelligence, the only delinquent among four siblings old enough to be delinquent, who for years had been engaging in such severe delinquency as

The Delinquents

larceny and burglary as well as many minor offenses, in spite of having received frequent beatings and having been held on numerous occasions in the detention home and sent to institutions.

To put it differently, we have not even classified as neurotic those cases in which we came to know that the antisocial conduct was based on deep emotional dissatisfactions or mental conflicts unless there were accompanying definite neurotic manifestations. The "neurotic character" of the psychoanalytic classification is another story hardly to be dealt with here.

The diagnosed neurotics and psychoneurotics exhibited such symptoms as tics and mannerisms, hypochondria, marked fears and anxieties, hysterical vomiting, sleep and food peculiarities, obsessive ideas, or compulsive types of behavior. Among several who had engaged in homosexual practices we diagnosed one case as a homosexual personality because from early years he had strongly showed his tendency to sexual inversion and in physical configuration clearly belonged to the type.

In the last few years better criteria for diagnosing neuroticism and personality abnormalities have begun to be developed and at the same time psychiatry has become more aware of the dynamic factors which may produce neurotics and delinquents.[4] In spite of all that is still lacking in biological knowledge of the constitutional and functional background of abnormal behavior we are making advancement in the sharpening of our concepts. This is reflected in the careful classification which this study presents, made possible by prolonged observation and accumulation of data.

From the standpoint of prognosis concerning recidivism or even the mental health and social adjustment of these in-

---

4. See, for example, *Roots of Crime,* Franz Alexander and William Healy, New York, 1935.

dividuals, one can hardly exaggerate the importance of our findings.[5] With few exceptions the above cases have responded to treatment by families, court officials, and social agencies with further evidences of erratic and delinquent conduct. They have already been expensive to society and bid fair to become even more costly. What was or was not accomplished by the treatment that we attempted to direct through available resources appears later in our discussion of treatment and outcomes.

Personality Characteristics

GREAT *restlessness or overactivity* was frequently reported by parents, teachers, and others to be an habitual characteristic of the delinquent; in not a few cases it was observed by members of our staff. This has led us to examine carefully our records for this kind of behavior manifestation as exhibited to a degree clearly above the norm for childhood or adolescence. Because the following terms are often used together or evidently interchangeably, it seems highly probable that they all represent one general type of psychophysical expression of personality tendencies and, therefore, can rightfully be placed in one category. An individual could evidently be fairly characterized as extremely active, overrestless or overlively, as showing uncontrolled, uninhibited physical impulses (sometimes he is spoken of as being very aggressive), or as being excessively fond of excitement. In this category, and we repeat that we are enumerating merely those who showed this type of behavior to a most unusual or abnormal degree, we found one third of our total number of delinquents, 53 cases. We are forced to agree with some other students of behavior problems that hyperactivity

5. It may be by chance and possibly in the Detroit group through some special selection, arising because of Judge Reid's desire for help in puzzling cases, that the figures for these deviations loom large. Certainly the percentage is greater than in any series of delinquents that we have previously studied.

on the part of children is strongly related to the appearance of delinquency.[6] In our series no other single personality characteristic is found in any exaggerated degree so frequently.

To be sure, 19 of the above cases fall in the group of those diagnosed as neurotic or as personality deviates, but even so the factor of hyperactivity, etc., may have much to do with their becoming delinquent.

A highly debatable question is whether or not such uninhibited behavior as we have just enumerated is caused by structural or functional peculiarities of the central nervous system, by obscure malfunctioning of other organs, or is the expression of emotional tensions occurring at even an early period of life as the result of situational experiences. We have carefully analyzed our developmental histories and find rather definite data about the age of onset of the overactivity, etc., in 38 cases. In 25 of these the characteristic was shown at least before school age, and in a few it was definitely noted even in infancy. Brain trauma or chorea apparently accounted for 6 other cases and 3 began to show the phenomenon in adolescence without known cause. Evidently the question cannot be answered, but from some special observations we are forced to conclude that there is evidence that emotional thwartings and dissatisfactions, themselves dating back to very early years, may be the inciting cause of hyperactivity. In reviewing the family relationships of the overrestless cases we discovered that the vast majority had highly disturbing emotional situations in the family life. But both this and the concomitancy of hyperactivity and delinquency are more sharply defined when delinquents and non-delinquents are contrasted.

Concerning *display of emotions* as indicated by moodiness, temper outbursts, irritability, etc., we can state that

6. See, for example, "Hyper-Activity in Children Having Behavior Disorders," by A. T. Childers, *American Journal of Orthopsychiatry,* July, 1935.

about 65 per cent of the delinquents seemed to show normal emotional balance or control. Some, about 7 per cent, appeared unusually stolid in outward expression of their emotions. With all that we know about the handicaps and dissatisfactions and inner conflicts of these delinquents, the above figures demonstrate that such objective signs cannot be relied on to reveal the true facts about feelings that reactively tend to provoke delinquent behavior.

The *ethical conceptions and sensibilities* of these delinquents naturally had much interest for us. Our inquiries showed that in the great majority their ideas of what is right or wrong were pretty much those of the ordinary run of young people. Only about 25 per cent of the cases, we estimated, demonstrated any marked lack of appreciation of the wrongfulness of their delinquent conduct, and even then in almost no case was there any attempt at justification of their behavior. The fact of the matter is plain: young people enter into delinquency commonly not with any deliberate rejection of ethical standards nor as a rational enterprise. Later on in life when criminalistic skills are acquired and material gains result and when current dishonesties are cynically viewed and criminal companionships formed, the story may be different. In all of our experience we have known of comparatively few cases, although we have known some, in which the young person, say before 17 years of age, has thought out for himself a life plan which includes delinquency as, for him, a justifiable line of action.

Conscious *inferiority feelings* were plainly enough evidenced in about a third of our series. We could make no satisfactory study of whether or not the inferiority feeling preceded the delinquency or was the outcome of scoldings and punishments following misbehavior. This statement, however, by no means covers the dynamic issues in cases where inadequacies really existed but were not verbalized or where inferiorities were unconsciously felt. In some cases, as we well

The Delinquents

know, delinquency may represent an unconscious attempt to compensate for inferiority. More of this later.

To assay our material in terms of *extroversion and introversion* was not a very satisfactory task—it is not so easy to classify children and, furthermore, most individuals seemed to be of mixed type. We could discern that about an equal number, some 15 per cent, did show, on the whole, marked introvert or extrovert characteristics. Either type, then, may enter the ranks of delinquents.

This subject leads us to mention *phantasy life*. For whatever it is worth, we can state that nearly one third of the delinquents were reported to be notable day-dreamers. Whether they were mainly brooding on their troubles in life or were phantasying about delinquency or other adventures, pleasures or heroics, would be hard to answer. We, however, know that the pleasures and gains of delinquent exploits do with some children play a considerable part in their phantasy life.

That delinquency is mainly the expression of peculiar *selfishness* engaged in for the delinquent's own pleasure at the expense of anyone else or anything else is an opinion held by some. Our findings weigh against this; we could not find that those we studied were in any considerable proportion especially pleasure loving youngsters.

Interests and habits we know a great deal about not only as given in the statistical summary, but we also had intimate knowledge of church attendance, club affiliations, and the use of leisure. All these, however, are only to be seen in any true perspective as related to their conduct tendencies when paralleled with like data concerning the non-delinquent siblings.

Social Adjustments

It seemed of great importance to ascertain the adjustments of delinquents to the primary social groups, the home and the school. It certainly was of great significance to find that in not more than 20 per cent were the family relationships of the delinquent reasonably satisfactory. Love for the father was expressed or evidenced in only about one fifth of the cases. In very numerous instances the child was either thoroughly indifferent to him or resented him.

It was to be expected that we should discover evidences that the mother was loved more often, but strong affection for her could only be detected in somewhat less than half the cases. Such thwartings of the normal needs of childhood as these attitudes represent offer clues to deeper understandings of fundamental sources of antisocial conduct.

Then what about the situational adjustment of the delinquents in their school life? We need say little here about their scholarship record; that correlates fairly well with their intelligence levels except as they were retarded on account of frequent change of residence or many absences (60 per cent were recorded as truants). Much more significant was it to find that no less than 40 per cent of these young people expressed a marked dislike of school and 13 per cent said they hated some one or more of their teachers. In the light of such a discovery as this delinquency still remains a great challenge to school people.

Thinking of these youthful thwartings and dissatisfactions as possibly forming a basis for the growth of delinquent trends, we combined our findings about the home and school situation. The startling fact emerged that in no less than 75 per cent there was evidence of marked dislike either of school or of father or of mother. Such a large percentage seems vastly significant as indicating the part that the emotional life plays in the genesis of delinquency.

Emotional Adjustments

THEN are delinquents obviously unhappy children? Very many of our series were registered as irritable, tempery, antagonistic, embittered, cynical, moody, sensitive, and unhappy—we take these terms at random from the case records. But every worker with children knows very well that the judgment of happiness from external signs is difficult; a child may appear happy and pleased in one situation and the reverse in other relationships, or may fluctuate from time to time. Much better judgment concerning fundamental unhappinesses is to be obtained through knowing the specific dissatisfactions which have existed in immediate life situations.

In order to have as valid a picture as possible of the emotional disturbances that may be factors in the origin of delinquent trends, we may here give the types of dissatisfactions which we came to know existed. Though we present this most important subject with more detail in our chapters comparing delinquents and controls, it is valuable to emphasize our findings for the whole series.

Among the 143 delinquents accepted as cases for treatment, major emotional disturbances were discovered to exist in 131 instances (92 per cent). Our studies of these delinquents and their family lives show:

Feelings of being rejected, unloved, or insecure in affectional relationships—53 cases.

Deep feelings of being thwarted in self-expression and other self-satisfactions—45 cases.

Marked feelings of inadequacy or inferiority in some situations or activities—62 cases.

Emotional disturbance about family disharmonies, discipline, etc.—43 cases.

Great persisting sibling jealousy or rivalry—43 cases.

Deep-set internal emotional conflicts—19 cases.

An unconscious sense of guilt and feeling of need for punishment—discovered in 11 cases.

The delinquent behavior of the remaining 12 cases can readily be accounted for by factors other than emotional disturbances. Particularly prominent in these instances is the influence of bad companions in high delinquency areas and low ethical standards in family life.

It, then, has become clear to us that, though in popular and often in more technical discussion the effect of environmental stresses is so tremendously emphasized, only a small proportion of delinquency can be interpreted alone in terms of external circumstances. The evidence for this is obtained when delinquents are thoroughly enough known so that their emotional or feeling life is revealed. To be sure, since delinquency is the individual's reaction to his environment, in all instances life situations and social pressures do play a part in the production of delinquency. But the above findings and particularly our later comparisons of delinquents and nondelinquents prove conclusively that vastly more dynamic is the subjective side of the delinquent's life, his feelings, attitudes, and mental content. Our new orientations of the specific causations of delinquency have been evolved from these more thorough studies of delinquents and their families.

STATISTICS FOR 153 DELINQUENTS ORIGINALLY TAKEN FOR STUDY

(For additional data see Chapter V)

Sex
- Boys — 130 cases
- Girls — 23 cases

Age
- Less than 12 years — 27 per cent
- Between 12 and 15 years — 42 per cent
- Over 15 years — 31 per cent

Position in family
- Oldest child — 25 per cent
- Youngest child — 12 per cent
- Having older and younger siblings — 63 per cent

Illegitimate children — 7 cases

The Delinquents

Age of first delinquency	
At 8 years or earlier	48 per cent
Between 8 and 12 years	30 per cent
After 12 years	22 per cent
Court cases	146 cases
In hands of police but not in court	3 cases
Not court or police cases	4 cases
Court cases	
Recidivism	60 per cent
First appearance	40 per cent
Actual first offense	5 per cent
Offenses	
Petty pilfering, including stealing from 5 and 10 cent stores	71 per cent
Serious shoplifting	7 per cent
Breaking and entering	33 per cent
Larceny, including automobile stealing	57 per cent
Considerable truancy	58 per cent
Running away from home	36 per cent
Staying out all night	16 per cent
Heterosexual offenses	13 per cent
Serious setting fire	5 cases
Ringing false fire alarm	2 cases
Attempt at suicide	2 cases
Attempt to commit murder	1 case
Manslaughter	2 cases
Drunkenness	3 cases
Carrying weapon	1 case
Assault and battery	2 cases
Malicious mischief	5 cases
Physical deviations	
More than 3 ins. short for age norms	23 per cent
More than 10 per cent underweight for age-height norms	9 per cent
More than 20 per cent overweight for age-height norms	6 per cent
Marked visual defect	17 per cent

More than slightly carious teeth	31 per cent
Diseased tonsils	18 per cent

Mental test findings
I.Q. 110 or above	11 per cent
I.Q. 90 to 110	53 per cent
I.Q. 80 to 90	27 per cent
I.Q. 72 to 80	7 per cent
I.Q. 69 to 71	2 per cent

	Approximate Percentages
Special Personality Characteristics	
Overrestless, overactive	34 per cent
Very gregarious	50 per cent
Tending to be solitary	15 per cent
Normal emotional balance or control	65 per cent
Stolid in expression of emotions	7 per cent
Temper outbursts, marked irritability, etc.	28 per cent
Normal in expression of ethical conceptions concerning conduct	75 per cent
Obtuse in ethical conceptions	25 per cent
Conscious inferiority feelings	33 per cent
Marked extravert tendencies	15 per cent
Marked intravert tendencies	15 per cent
Notably day-dreamers	30 per cent

Habits and Interests
Strong interest in reading	50 per cent
Strong interest in active games and athletics	52 per cent
Much attendance at movies (more than twice a week)	55 per cent
Much smoking	30 per cent
Extreme masturbation	25 per cent
Associated with delinquent companions	70 per cent

Social relationships
Good general family relationships	20 per cent
Father loved	20 per cent
Mother loved	48 per cent
School strongly disliked	40 per cent
Dislike of teacher	13 per cent
Marked dislike either of school or of father or mother	75 per cent

CHAPTER V

STUDIES OF DELINQUENTS AND NON-DELINQUENTS IN THE SAME FAMILIES

Comparison of Personalities

WHY in the same family is one child delinquent and another not delinquent?

If so many of the circumstances and attitudes revealed by these studies of family life are deleterious and provocative of delinquency—and who can doubt that they are active influences—the wonder is that no more of the children are delinquent. The rational expectation would be that siblings in these families might more or less equally show delinquent tendencies. Proponents of theories about individual biological and constitutional variations find some support in the cases of neurotic and abnormal personality that we have discussed, but these latter are comparatively few in number. Various other single-cause theories can be and have been advanced, for example religious or educational, but a scientifically conducted inquiry must take deep soundings in all directions and weigh all facts that can be ascertained.

At any rate the dissimilar behavior of different children in the same family forces the above common-sense query which we have many times put to ourselves. And so why not study the non-delinquent for the purpose of discovering how he escaped being an offender! Now for the first time this research has offered opportunity for delving far enough into the lives of young people so that scientifically ordered comparisons may be made and deductions drawn therefrom. The goal is better understandings of the origins of delinquent tendencies. Whether such understandings will further efficacious preventive treatment is for the future to determine.

We deal with 105 delinquents paired with non-delinquents including 8 pairs of twins—for convenience we may use the term "control" to designate the compared non-delinquent. In our attempt to study a non-delinquent sibling in every family a good many others were investigated but for various reasons were ruled out. They were not utilized as controls because they could not be compared with the delinquents in all aspects of the research. Not all those selected for controls were available for complete study, some were not fully willing to coöperate, and even after studying them we eliminated several pairs on account of too great disparity in their ages. Then a few, as we came to know them better, proved to have been recently delinquent themselves.

It is not to be supposed that none of the 105 individuals that finally formed the control series had ever transgressed. Considering the circumstances of many of them, that would be expecting too much; but, as we have already intimated, it is almost astounding to find that so few had at any time been offenders.

As a matter of fact our careful investigation shows that only 21 had ever been even so much as mildly delinquent—and if anything we are slightly overstating the number. Of these, 10 had sometime earlier been truant and 9 had engaged in petty stealing, one was in a rather serious boyish mischief affair when a barn was pulled down. Only 2 or 3 had at any time been somewhat implicated in an offense that amounted to much. Just one had been in the juvenile court because his heavily delinquent brother and another boy had induced him to go into a shop which they robbed. He maintained that he was merely "pulled in" and his brother completely exonerated him, stating that it was quite unfair for him to have been taken to court. These few who had ever broken the rules of society had not done so at all recently. We feel convinced that this small amount of delinquency represents the real facts; the corroborative accounts given

The Personalities of Delinquents and Controls 55

by parents, school people, the controls themselves, and their delinquent siblings ring true.

If we consider their life situations, the contrast between the conduct tendencies of the delinquents and the controls is amazing and the instances where the individual had not gone on with more delinquency are almost more striking than when it had been entirely avoided. The causes for this freedom from or desistance from delinquency prove to be some of the most interesting of our findings.

We regard it as most fortunate that the research with its limited working period finally can show such a considerable number of pairs which have been studied with care and followed by parallel methods in families where social and psychiatric treatment was undertaken. The work done on this feature of the original project represents a huge task.

Comparison of Objective Data

FROM a wealth of material we may first offer the main objective data,[1] reserving for the next four chapters discussion of the emotional life and relationships within the family group.

Age—Concerning relative ages of the pairs, we desired wherever possible to take for the control the sibling of the same sex as the delinquent and nearest in age—preference being for the next older because through added years the control might be able to give a more reliable comparative account of himself and of the delinquent. But families were not constructed to our order and so we had to take the control that was available. Finally we had almost exactly the same number of older controls as of younger, the younger ones being each near enough the delinquent in age to have possibly been under the same influences and to have shown the same reactions. Hence any contrast in age distributions cannot account for the behavior differences.

1. For detailed statistics see appendix at end of chapter.

The numerical position of the child in the family and the instances where there was a step-parent or an adoptive parent shows slight and consequently non-significant differences for the compared groups.

Sex—For the 92 boys and 13 girls who formed the contrasted series of delinquents we took 81 boys and 24 girls for controls. In the 13 cases of boys and 2 of girls where we took a control of the opposite sex it was because there was no other that answered the requirements. This was not ideal but was the best we could do and proved to be of no great disadvantage because nearly all of the girls who formed controls for the boys lived under conditions where they might readily have been delinquent and indeed in some instances had sisters who were delinquent.

Physical Status—Biologically, as evidenced by a thorough physical examination, the two groups presented very marked similarities. Enumerated deviations in terms of pathological conditions were not far from the same for both delinquents and controls. Half or more of both proved to be in good physical condition and marked physical assets were shown by 10 delinquents and 16 controls, the individual being unusually well built and strong, some being very attractive in appearance.

Even though fine anthropometric measurements were not undertaken, the examiners carefully registered stigmata, deformities, and any structural peculiarities. The mass figures are astonishingly similar for both groups, about 5 per cent. Of course this does not mean that in an individual case such a deviation may not be a factor; it is always a matter of the child's reactions to his handicap.

Developmental History—Detailed inquiry into the developmental history of the children brought forth some remarkable contrasts. Information was obtained that can be considered fairly satisfactory and reliable for 100 pairs. The enumerated deviations from the ordinarily considered healthy norms for antenatal conditions, birth, and for postnatal development when totaled as separate items show a great difference—170 developmental deviations for the delinquents as compared to 74 for the controls.

The most marked contrasts, namely, those items which showed considerably more than 50 per cent difference and were not numerically negligible were:

	Delinquents	Controls
Much worry during pregnancy	10	3
Very sickly pregnancy	13	6
Cross, fussy babyhood	14	5
Difficult toilet habit-training	31	13
Much underweight in early childhood	12	5
Many or severe illnesses	28	8
Severe head injuries	5	0

It can be seen at once that many more of the delinquents than of the controls had been subject to interference with healthy normal development. The relationship however between health conditions and behavior tendencies is not easy to determine. One might speculate, for example, about the significance of severe illness—as consequent to the disease was there organically caused irritability or restlessness, or was the child spoiled or overprotected on account of illness, or did he through illness acquire specially demanding and selfish attitudes?

Concerning brain pathology, as we stated in the previous chapter the findings for severe head injuries are significant. Then, though we obtained for only two delinquents any history of an illness that in itself suggested encephalitis (particularly epidemic encephalitis, "sleeping sickness") yet with the knowledge of the relation of this disease, so often undiagnosed, to behavior disorders we may allow ourselves to suspect that it was more frequent. Certain other cases behaved much the same as those who are known to have suffered from encephalitis.

To complete our story of the developmental histories, we have reckoned up all the instances in which distinctly good health, except for very mild attacks of the diseases of childhood, was specifically reported—delinquents 44, controls 75. Certainly again the balance is weighted considerably in favor of the controls.

Personality Deviations—The importance of abnormal personality, neurosis or early psychosis in relation to delinquency is not to be denied—we may again refer the reader to the preceding chapter for our discussion of the subject. The great point to be brought out here is the tremendous contrast between the delinquents and controls. The former include 25 instances where a definite diagnosis was made in terms of one of the above categories and among the controls there were only 2 diagnosable by the same criteria. Added to this, such a probable diagnosis was offered for 5 delinquents and no control. Thus the rôle that personality deviations play in the genesis of delinquent behavior stands out most strongly. When a young individual abnormal according to any of the above classifications, and hence lacking in normal inhibitory powers, encounters the stressful conditions and thwartings that most of our delinquents had to meet through family life, companionship, or school failure and develops from any source ideas of delinquency, evidently delinquent conduct is almost bound to ensue.

If this is true we are interested to know how even the two personality deviates among the controls avoided becoming delinquent. One was a heavily introverted, withdrawing schizoid older adolescent who would not associate with companions as his younger brother did, preferring rather to spend most of his time at home in phantasy, meanwhile accepting his mother's support. The other was an aggressive, embittered, suspicious, touchy youth, inclined to be a radical, showing extreme obstinacy and bad temper in a large overcrowded family of distinctly fine ideals. As we have continued our contact with the family, we have found that this peculiarly behaving youth, earlier "a devil at home and a saint outside," has done well at work and has greatly mitigated his home attitudes. We are now inclined to question our previous diagnosis and to consider his behavior as representing jealousy and spite reactions largely fostered in a naturally aggressive individual who was under the influence of a dominating interfering grandmother. Perhaps maturity itself has tended to sober and stabilize him.

Physical Habits—Peculiar physical habits were regarded by us as possibly being indicators of internal tensions, whether genetically related to delinquency or the result of it. Counting as separate items food idiosyncrasies, sleep disturbances, much nail biting, thumb sucking, and other nervous mannerisms, exhibited at the period when we were making our study, we found the total twice as large for the delinquents as for the controls. However, none of these habits had a frequency rating high enough to be in the least diagnostic for the group and more than one of the items was sometimes scored for the same individual. But the fact that 44 delinquents as against 24 controls exhibited such peculiar habits indicates a tendency for the former to show more signs of nervous tension than the non-delinquent siblings. The same may be said of speech defects—7 delinquents exhibiting this difficulty and only one of the controls.

Enuresis, reported by many observers as a habit frequently found among delinquents, shows in great contrast for the two groups. Taking arbitrarily the criterion that habitual enuresis, not "an occasional accident," after eight years of age is very significant and probably not then due to lack of training, we found it displayed in 22 instances among the delinquents and in 4 controls. Nowadays it is well recognized that there is psychological significance in most instances of protracted bed wetting—whether the trouble be interpreted as a masturbatory substitute, an attention-getting device, or a revenge phenomenon. In our cases where most often it was continued well into the second decade of life it seems most likely to be allied to some, often unconscious, emotional disturbance.

Though the percentages for these physical habits are not great yet they are indicators that the delinquent tends to be more unstable and more uncontrolled than the non-delinquent sibling. Perhaps this is well enough recognized and our figures were to be expected.

Mental Abilities—Somewhat to our surprise, since we are still probably a little under the spell of the Aristotelian dictum that good conduct is strongly correlated with good intelligence, the mental age-levels of the two groups prove to be only slightly contrasting. Skilful psychological testing shows that well within the limits of normal mental ability, according to standard age-level tests, there were 98 of the delinquents and 94 controls. Superior ability was demonstrated by 14 delinquents as compared to 18 controls. No comment on these findings seems necessary; the figures speak for themselves.

We were interested in having our psychologists give a special test for apperceptive abilities, Pictorial Completion Test II, because it was thought possible that differences in the capacity for this type of reasoning ability might occur in the two groups. The results failed to show much—only 10 per cent of the controls did distinctly better than the delinquents.

Nor when we tried to discover special mental disabilities by psychological and educational tests—such as disabilities for reading or language acquirement or for rote learning—did we find anything but marked similarity between the two groups. Here it may be of interest to mention that in neither group was there any clear-cut instance of reading disability.

The same similarity was recorded for acquirement of general information as estimated by special tests.

The Personalities of Delinquents and Controls 61

Then instead of the delinquent showing relatively more ability to work manually with concrete problems, and particularly with tests for mechanical ability, it was the other way around—the controls did somewhat better.

Looking for special abilities that might be thought of as having been the saving grace for many controls, leading them to have special interests and pleasures in achievement, we found that no more of them than of the delinquents demonstrated on tests any such abilities. However, it should be noted that a certain number of the controls, perhaps without any more marked abilities than their delinquent siblings, did develop special interests in manual occupations or in art and music which helped them greatly to gain satisfactions that outweighed or prevented feelings of being thwarted by life situations and probably averted temptations to resort to delinquency for satisfactions.

Reckoning it all up, it appears that the great amount of carefully conducted and intensive psychological testing resulted, quite unexpectedly, in establishing no signs of differentiation between the mental equipment of the delinquents and the controls in our series.

School Records—School records were obtained with much care. We found that almost all the non-attendance of the controls was occasioned by illness or changing residence. But about 60 per cent of the delinquents were out-and-out truants, with evasions of attendance running as high as one year in one case. The scholarship record was of course affected by this but not to the extent that might be surmised. Definitely poor scholarship was registered for only 34 per cent of the delinquents, as against 18 per cent of the controls. So by no means are all delinquents found to be recorded as poor students. Partly to check up on this we gave school achievement tests and found considerably below the standards for grade or age only 20 per cent of the delinquents—and 5 per cent of the controls.

Furthermore we were interested to learn the extent of grade retardation for the two groups as it might have bearing on unfavorable school attitudes; we were again surprised to discover no marked differences. Thus, though we know there were exceptions, for the series as a whole the age-grade placement seems to have very little relationship to the tremendous amount of school dissatisfaction which is part of the picture of the emotional life of the delinquents as compared to the controls.

School Attitudes—About 40 per cent of the delinquents expressed marked dislike for school in general and 13 per cent marked dislike for some teacher. A mere 4 per cent of the controls evinced any such dislikes. We also discovered that 14 per cent of the delinquents considered themselves unpopular or teased at school—and none of the controls. We are not passing judgment on the causes for any of this but the facts are most striking.

While these school attitudes do not seem to show overwhelmingly in scholarship records and less in school achievement tests and in age-grade placement, they must be closely correlated with the great extent of truancy in which the delinquents indulged. The question with which we open this chapter might here be paraphrased: Why, coming from the same family, is one child truant and another not? If adequate attempts were made to answer this specific query, what an opportunity there would be for school people to detect and check impending serious delinquent tendencies!

Comparison of Personality Characteristics

Dynamic—Turning now to comparison of clearly revealed personality characteristics, we begin with dynamic qualities. In the chapter, The Delinquents, it was stated that a third of the total number showed *hyperactivity* or allied manifestations. How do the 105 pairs compare in this respect?

In the first place, as definitely more active, restless, ener-

The Personalities of Delinquents and Controls 63

getic, or as showing more uninhibited behavior than the controls, 68 of the delinquents were recorded. Only 11 of the delinquents were less active, etc., than the controls. This contrast is accentuated by finding that observers very frequently describe the latter in strongly negative terms from a dynamic standpoint. Many controls, 41 to be exact, were characterized as being subdued, retiring, quiet, inactive, placid, nonaggressive, not caring for adventure or excitement.

But the difference in the two groups comes out strongest when we consider the exhibition of dynamic characteristics to an extent above the normal. Hyperactivity, overrestlessness, extreme physical aggressiveness, great impulsiveness, or some allied manifestation was recorded for 46 delinquents. *Not one control was so characterized.*

We gave in the previous chapter some further data that we gathered for this special study of energy output and control—the age of onset of overactivity, etc., and possible genetic implications. Here we may add that information on the 46 delinquents showing habitual uncontrolled behavior proved that 38 had lived in family situations where their emotional relationships had been distinctly depriving, thwarting, or otherwise unsatisfactory. For the 8 who had no special emotional thwartings in family life, the uninhibited behavior could be entirely accounted for by the fact that they all belonged to the group of abnormal personalities.

Social—The social characteristics of delinquents always appear important to consider because so little delinquency is engaged in without companionship or gang connections. Without tackling the moot question of whether or not there is in the human species any "herd instinct," we can discuss gregarious proclivities—taking the accepted definition of *gregariousness* as meaning a strong inclination to associate with the crowd. This is clearly more prevalent in the delinquents than in the controls. We found that 31 delinquents were definitely associating with delinquent crowds but in only very few instances were these organized gangs in the sense that they had definitive leadership or a gang name. In the vast majority of the remainder the delinquent fellowship was confined to one or two boon companions. Some few engaged in delinquency alone. The crowd associations undoubtedly represented an expression of the individual's social urges, although we discovered that in a few instances it was just out of the impulse to offset dissatisfactions by doing something forbidden or desperate that the individual deliberately sought out a delinquent crowd; we suspect this may have been more common than we knew.

At the other extreme, some 16 delinquents had few or no friends, tending markedly to be solitary in both their general interests and in their delinquencies.

Now only 11 of the controls were clearly gregarious, that is, participate in crowd companionship, although the majority had a small number of friends. That some 23 controls definitely avoided companionship is not to be wondered at; in their social situation it was part of their defense against getting into trouble. We know that even a greater number were satisfied with quiet home pursuits that would lead them to have very little companionship.

Some interesting results were obtained from the inquiry into social characteristics according to an *ascendance-submission* scale. Considered as ascendant traits were a marked showing of insubordination, wilful disobedience, defiance, desire to dominate, self-assertiveness, active resentfulness, all or any of which indicated the desire of the individual to control his environment. As belonging to the category of submissive tendencies we regarded instances where the individual was observed to be or reported to be unusually subdued, very obedient and compliant, not resentful, meek, easily conforming—characteristics which proved their ready acceptance of situations, good or bad. Showing ascendant tendencies we found 28 per cent of the delinquents and 6 per cent of the controls; distinctly submissive tendencies, delinquents only 2 per cent and controls 15 per cent.

Emotional—In such display of the emotions as frequently varying moods, often displayed sulkiness, excessive bad temper, etc., divergencies between the two groups are shown but without any large differences if we allow for the peculiar behavior manifestations of the abnormal personalities. The large majority of both delinquents and controls were not recognized as habitually presenting anything but normal emotional poise. So for the most part the delinquents' dissatisfactions, which we know many of them felt, were not manifested by observed outward expressions of emotional disturbance. The frequently hidden emotional difficulties revealed only through psychiatric exploration is a subject dealt with in the next chapter.

The *extrovert-introvert* personality categories are always intriguing, but even on the third rechecking of our material for this point we find classifications exceedingly difficult. (The standardized extrovert-introvert questionnaires were not applicable to our groups, with all the differences in ages and cultural backgrounds that existed.) Most individuals unquestionably are of mixed type, the so-called ambiverts, but we did find clear exemplars of introversion and extroversion. These number less than ten for each type in both delinquents and controls. Perhaps it might have been anticipated that more of the delinquents would prove to be extroverts, with outgoing qualities making for ready contacts with the more vicious elements in their environment. Undoubtedly to a considerable extent extrovert qualities of even ambiverts are thus utilizable in the search for compensatory satisfactions but, naturally, we also found controls readily making contacts with companions and interests that evidently played a definite part in preventing delinquency.

Inferiority Feelings—Confining ourselves here to the descriptive level of personality characteristics, rather than making, as we do later, deeper soundings into the problem of whether delinquent behavior is not often compensatory for hidden or unconscious sensing of inferiority, we have enumerated those who overtly exhibited or expressed marked feelings of inferiority. This was found in 38 delinquents and only in 4 controls. Whether or not social disapproval consequent upon delinquency was any effective cause in producing the feeling of inferiority was rarely clear but certainly in a considerable number we discovered that a sense of inadequacy preceded the delinquency and tended to precipitate it. And then at least for these 38 cases it is evident that delinquent exploits did not bolster up the ego to the extent that the feeling of inferiority disappeared. We speak of this particularly because in some instances it has come out plainly that the individual engaged in delinquency partly to prove to himself that he could be as daring, courageous, and adequate as others whom he admired. The term "masculine protest" could well be applied to such instances.

That the controls expressed so little feeling of inadequacy or inferiority is not to be explained by the amount of their relative achievement. Indeed not a few of them, some 29, were quiet home-bodies obtaining ordinary satisfactions through family attachments and simple pursuits. If the question of personality evaluation is at issue, many of these could be regarded as demonstrating to varying degrees negative or inferior qualities, even though they gave no outward expression of feeling inadequate.

Ethical Sensibilities—An attempt to compare the ethical conceptions or sensibilities of the two groups leads only to the following conclusions: many of the controls, as will be seen later when we discuss the reasons they gave for not being delinquent, expressed strong conceptions of the values of being "good" and certainly all seemed to display some feeling about right and wrong conduct. Then among the delinquents, we found not more than half a dozen who could be conceived of as being conscienceless, even about the kind of delinquency in which they engaged. Perhaps we might think in these terms of two young thieving boys whose poverty-stricken and dishonest parents were willing recipients of their loot (the controls being afraid to steal "because of the cops"); also of a heavily sex-delinquent boy who had been inducted into many affairs of this sort; and of a pair of older girls who since early childhood had been deeply immersed in various kinds of delinquency. Quite to the contrary we discovered clear evidences of much remorse and guilt on the part of not a few severe offenders. As a very rough estimation we would say that not more than a fourth of the delinquents were without considerable feeling about the wrongfulness of their behavior. And it would be quite untrue to state that any, even the abnormal personalities, did not have knowledge of the nature and quality of their actions to the extent that they were unaware that they were doing wrong—the legalistic conception of irresponsibility. Thus we had no reason to believe that any of the cases were "moral imbeciles"—a term the value of which we much question.

The Thought Content—Doubtless, could we have learned about it in a considerable number of instances, the content of the *day-dreams* of our groups would have proved interesting to compare. Day-dreams or phantasies, the free wandering of thought untrammeled by considerations of reality, represent for all human beings, especially during youth, the unbidden expression of feelings and desires that are potent in forming conduct tendencies. Though our inquiries met with some success, in most instances it was very difficult to obtain verbalization of phantasies. As all psychiatrists who work with children and adolescents know, frequently there is great resistance to any exploration of phantasy life—the individual feels it as his private possession not to be violated.

Some dozen cases revealed extensive day-dreaming about delinquency, picturing themselves as being enterprising adepts in youthful criminality or as obtaining revenge through delinquency.

This brings us to the larger matter of the whole *ideational life* of the two groups. Since the thought-life is not easily searched out, a thoroughgoing study of ideas held would have required years of work. As it was, we did get these young people to express themselves about many things that seemed important to them and through this they uncovered some reasons for their behavior tendencies and revealed many of their emotional attitudes, but a comparative study of all the important thought trends of the different individuals is quite another story.

The immediate causative background of delinquent behavior is composed not alone of insufficient satisfactions in socialized "good" behavior for a dissatisfied individual but also of what has been going on in thought-life concerning delinquency. Through his fund of ideas it has seemed to the individual that somehow delinquency would be a gain for him— in material returns or in adventure or in prestige won. Very few indeed, if any, enter into delinquency as the result of a newborn impulse, without previously having had thought about it. There is almost universally some period of incubation of such ideas, generally not thought out to definite conclusions concerning action, but still recurring as part of the mental content. An educative or assimilative process has been going on, usually under the stimulus of some environmental source or sources, whereby the individual learns about delinquency, its forms and techniques, as he might become informed or educated about, we will say, tree climbing. He learns about it through seeing it or hearing or reading about it.

Without pretending that we are giving or that we know the whole story, we have positive evidence from accounts

The Personalities of Delinquents and Controls

given by delinquents themselves that in a full third there had been much loading of the thought-life with ideas of delinquency—and often this had been going on for years. This particular educative process generally began with information received from youthful comrades—two were taught by older criminals. Some said they had learned about delinquency from a mixture of sources, for example, the communications of delinquent companions, perhaps even observations of them in delinquency, plus ideas derived from detective or crime stories and the movies. Some had given really planful thought to possible delinquent exploits—a couple of youthful burglars told of making studies and sketches of the places they entered. Reinforcements of ideas already entertained frequently assailed the individual through further contact with delinquent companions—some gave accounts of much talk about delinquency in detention homes or other institutions. Or further observations of opportunities or of actual delinquencies perpetrated, or further reading or movies gave new suggestions.

Whether from such repetitious reinforcements from outside sources or from the forming of thought channels that probably signify neural canalizations, the frequency and insistency of thoughts about delinquency certainly in some instances mounted almost into being mental obsessions—the individual could not seem successfully to combat the force of his recurrent ideas.

To be sure, the controls had many similar sources of information and unfortunate education open to them or thrust upon them, though possibly not so extensively, since they had vastly less association with delinquent companions. They all knew something about delinquency, had ideas about it, but these took no commanding part in their thoughts. Both of some pairs went to the same movies or read the same crime stories. In one good-sized family where there was only one delinquent, all including the parents read a great deal of such stuff. It was instructive to learn from some controls that for reasons phrased by themselves they had deliberately decided at one definite point in their careers to throw over ideas of delinquency and had succeeded in getting such ideas out of their minds. Knowing the possibilities of delinquency, they felt there were other and greater satisfactions for them; they sensed that delinquency would not answer their needs. With the development of ideas about delinquency it is as with the whole educational process: what is really absorbed and made part of one's thought-life depends on how one, particularly emotionally, is already prepared to be interested.

Interests and Activities—The interests of children as they are possibly related to the prevention of delinquency, or as they obviously have failed to prevent its development, would seem to be a matter of prime importance. We accumulated for comparative purposes quite a collection of data bearing on this, but of course the difficulty always was to know the real degree of interest or to have any criteria for determining it.

One thinks first of interest in religious instruction, in *church* or *Sunday school* affiliations. We found that 46 of the delinquents as against 64 controls were regular church or Sunday school attendants. Included among these are 7 delinquents and 10 controls who showed not a little religious feeling and attachment to the church. Some of the former even said they felt comfort in the church; many of them had been confirmed. Only 12 delinquents and 8 controls did not go to church or Sunday school at all.

These figures are difficult to interpret except as they show that church affiliations very frequently were not potent in combating stresses that make for the production of delinquency. This is not contradicting the fact, though the figures for attendance do not prove it, that the church is often influential in preventing delinquency—indeed in a few in-

The Personalities of Delinquents and Controls 71

stances controls directly told us this was so. Altogether we must come back to somewhat the same point we made about the school: pastors and Sunday school teachers usually know little of the lives and personal problems of the young people they are endeavoring to influence. The question arises as to whether they are well enough trained in understanding children's problems to be able to aid in solving them. Certain it is that most of our families had not been to their pastors about difficulties with their delinquent children, but among the few instances where parents had sought such assistance we know that advice to punish had in a few instances caused deep resentment on the part of the child, who, feeling that he was not understood, became bitter toward the church and estranged from it. There are exceptions, but from our experience we know that church authorities seem little concerned about playing an effective rôle as therapists for behavior disorders.

Concerning membership in *clubs*, whether those connected with a settlement house, church, or other supervised organizations such as the scouts, we found that almost twice as many of the delinquents as of the controls had such connections at some time prior to our acquaintance with them. It is not surprising that more of the delinquents had registered club connections, in view of the fact that they on the whole were more outgoing and active. But then we discovered that in many instances clubs had not represented a long continued interest; attendance was irregular or the activities soon ceased to be attractive. It is an open question whether specially trained leaders should or could do more for the prevention of delinquency by an individual approach supplementing their program of group activities. Furthermore, can delinquent careers often be headed off without establishing social case-work relationships with the families? Since so much support is being given to boys' clubs with the hope that they may check delinquency, thought should also be given to the possibility of satisfying fundamental needs through club interests.

Participation in active *sports* is often thought of as a preventive of delinquency but our studies show that more of the delinquents than of the controls engaged in swimming and skating or played football, baseball, etc. Indeed 15 of the delinquents were notably good at athletics, almost twice as many as of the controls.

Our investigation of *reading* interests gave surprising returns as we compared the delinquents and controls. Evidently considerably more of the delinquents were fond of reading and were even said to be great readers. As far as we could gather, the specific types of reading engaged in were rather similar for the two groups—both preferring adventure stories of the type found in the cheaper magazines, but yet it was noted that some of the delinquents read more widely than this and enjoyed really good books.

Interest in the *movies* was exhibited much more by the delinquents than the controls. We found that 33 of the former attended excessively, several times a week or whenever they could, sometimes staying to see a performance over and over again—while anything like the same excess of attendance was noted for only 10 controls. Regular attendance once or twice a week was the habit of 88 of the delinquents as against 42 controls. This marked difference between the groups must have its implications though it would require careful study in each and every case to ascertain them: did the movies merely offer a temporary escape from unpleasant situations and unhappiness, or to what extent did the pictures have a specifically pernicious influence? Only a few of the delinquents stated that they had derived ideas from gangster or other crime pictures upon which they definitely patterned their own delinquencies.

The special interests or *hobbies* of both groups included

some that w_e surprisingly good—music, drawing, handicrafts, acroba_ics, animal pets, etc.—and in total there was little difference between the two.

CERTAIN STATISTICS CONCERNING DELINQUENTS AND CONTROLS
(105 of each)

	Delinquents	Controls
Sex		
Boys	92	81
Girls	13	24
Age		
Cases older than controls	47	..
Cases younger than controls	50	..
Twins	8	8
Position in family		
Eldest	27	16
Youngest	11	15
In between	67	74
Parental status		
Both parents in home	77	78
One or both parents dead	15	17
Stepfather	8	8
Stepmother	4	4
Parents separated or divorced	11	10
Living in adoptive or foster home	3	5
Illegitimate	2	0
Physical conditions—at time of study		
Marked physical assets	10	16
Good physical condition. Absence of anything except perhaps very slight pathological conditions	52	68
Very tall—5 in. or more	4	0
Very short—5 in. or more	10	7
Overweight—more than 20%	3	1

	Delinquents	Controls
Underweight—more than 10%	3	9
Very premature sexual development	4	0
Retarded sexual development	5	1
Defective vision—more than slight	17	6
Slight strabismus	3	2
Marked strabismus	0	1
Otitis media	1	5
Moderately defective hearing	1	3
Markedly enlarged or diseased tonsils	20	12
Nasal obstruction	6	2
At least some badly carious teeth	27	19
Endocrine disorder	4	0
Phimosis	4	1
Very poor posture	3	0
Miscellaneous liabilities	7	3
Structural peculiarities, stigmata, or deformities	6	6

Developmental history (100 pairs)

	Delinquents	Controls
Unwanted child	11	6
Abortion attempted	3	0
Much worried pregnancy	10	3
Very sickly pregnancy	13	6
Premature birth	2	1
Very difficult delivery	12	5
Much underweight in early childhood	12	5
Very early bottle fed	10	8
Very late breast fed	7	4
Very difficult weaning	2	0
Cross fussy babyhood	14	5
Difficult sphincter training	31	13
Many illnesses or severe illness	28	8
Diseases of central nervous system	5	3
Otitis media	3	6
Severe head injury	5	0
Encephalitis	2	1
	170	74
History of distinctly good health	44	75
Enuresis after 8 years	22	4

The Personalities of Delinquents and Controls

Personality Deviations

	Delinquents			Controls
	Definite diagnosis	Probable diagnosis	Possible diagnosis	Definite diagnosis
Neurosis or neuropsychosis	10	2	1	..
Mild or early psychosis	4	2	1	..
Abnormal personality				
Constitutional inferior personality	2	..	..	..
Egocentric unstable personality	2	..	..	..
Schizoid personality	..	..	..	1
Unclassified	1	..	..	1
Post traumatic personality	3	..	..	..
Post encephalitic personality	1	1	..	..
Epileptic personality	1	..	..	..
Homosexual personality	1	..	1	..
Total	25	5	3	2

Physical Habits at Time of Study

	Delinquents	Controls
Food idiosyncrasies	13	6
Sleep idiosyncrasies	8	3
Excessive nail-biting, -picking, etc.	12	7
Thumb-sucking	5	0
Other nervous manifestations	12	8
Individuals showing any of above habits	44	24
Speech defects	7	1
Excessive masturbation	11	?
Excessive smoking	9	2

Mental age-levels—Delinquents and Controls

I.Q. above 110	14	18
I.Q. 90 to 110	55	60
I.Q. 80 to 90	29	16
I.Q. 72 to 80	4	8
I.Q. 69 to 71	3	..
I.Q. 64 to 70	..	3
	105	105

Results on Pictorial Completion Test II
(For 87 pairs)

	Delinquents	Controls
Score well above age-norm	33	42
Score about average	21	21
Score clearly below age-norm	33	24
	87	87

School status

Markedly below grade or age-level on school achievement tests	20	5
Definitely poor scholarship record	34	18
Age-grade placement		
I.Q. 90 or above, and 2 or more years retarded		
Of 69 delinquents—10 per cent		
Of 78 controls—9 per cent		
I.Q. below 90, and 2 or more years retarded		
Of 36 delinquents—39 per cent		
Of 27 controls—27 per cent		
Strong dislike of school in general	40	4
Strong dislike of some teacher	13	0
Regarded themselves as teased or unpopular at school	14	0
Repeated, often excessive truancy	60	0
Very rare truancy	..	10

Personality characteristics

Hyperactivity, overrestlessness, etc.	46	0
Definitely more active, restless, etc., than control	68	..
Less active than control	11	..
24 pairs about equal in above characteristics		
2 pairs incompletely known in these respects		
Control notably quiet, placid, subdued, etc.	..	41
Great urge for crowd companionship	31	11
Tendency to avoid companionship	16	23
Showing marked ascendant tendencies	28	6
Distinctly submissive tendencies	2	15
Normal emotional control	70	94

	Delinquents	Controls
Particularly stolid or unemotional	7	1
Extroverts	9	7
Introverts	9	7
Marked feelings of inferiority	38	4

Interests

	Delinquents	Controls
Regular attendants at church or Sunday school	46	64
Considerable religious feeling	7	10
Irregular church attendance	44	30
No church or Sunday school attendance	12	8
Prior club connections	47	28
Scout membership	9	3
Marked interest or activity in sports	73	57
Notable skill in athletics	15	8
Fond of reading	76	55
Among the above those characterized as being great readers	41	25
Regular—more than occasional—movie attendance	88	42
Among the above those who attended movies excessively	33	10

CHAPTER VI

COMPARISON OF DELINQUENTS AND CONTROLS IN RELATION TO FAVORABLE AND INIMICAL FAMILY SITUATIONS

TURNING from comparison of personalities, we pursue further our quest for whatever had contributed to make one child delinquent and another non-delinquent. In this chapter we attempt to differentiate some of the forces in family life that have been actively at play in the lives of delinquents as contrasted with controls, though as objectively seen the situation for both in a given family setting appeared to be the same.

Those Living in Family Situations Apparently Favorable

To begin with, one may reasonably ask why *any delinquents* came from family situations which were graded as apparently favorable. It will be remembered that in discussing "The Families" we used three discriminating categories of conditions of family life. Now 19 of these 105 delinquents compared with controls were living under conditions which according to these categories were evaluated as not inimical. Why, then, should these 19 have become delinquent? Was the family life in any way responsible?

In reviewing the characteristics of these delinquents it was remarkable to find that no less than 14 showed marked personality or psycho-physical deviations which certainly are to be regarded as playing a part in determining their behavior. (For detailed enumeration see appendix to chapter.) The delinquency of the other 5 represented either strong reactions to family restrictions or to loneliness and boredom, with one case of obsessive urge for reckless automobile driving.

But can we feel altogether satisfied with deriving an explanation of delinquency from physical or personality deviations even when neuroticism is involved? The well-known unstable behavior manifestation of neurotics or of abnormal personalities can hardly be regarded as sole causes of delinquency because we know that some individuals with the same personality disorders are not delinquent. Nor is every restricted, bored, or lonely boy an offender against the law.

As a matter of fact deeper study revealed in nearly every one of these 19 delinquents living under relatively favorable conditions the existence of emotional attitudes that were important factors in the development of the delinquent tendencies. We would have expected that the neurotics had intense affective disturbances but it was not immediately discernible that an endocrine case, coming from a family of the highest integrity, had engaged in various serious offenses because he, in the confusion of adolescence, had a profound feeling of not being understood and of being isolated in the family circle—delinquency appearing to offer compensatory satisfactions. Nor was it at first plain that a boy's desires for the thrills of exciting adventure, expressed in his excursions into shoplifting though he came from a fairly well-to-do family, were reactions to his feelings of loneliness and boredom, and that these in turn were based on his sense of being utterly rejected by his parents and siblings who were all so immersed in their own concerns that they left him almost entirely alone.

Still another example of what there may be below the surface of readily discerned facts was found in the case of the fifteen-year old boy who seemed to present a picture of almost an adolescent psychosis. Having a record of earlier model conduct, this boy entered into very serious delinquencies with an older criminal companion whom he had met during a runaway episode. The lad was in a tremendously ambivalent state of mind concerning his fixation on his mother, his protracted infantile desire for bestowal of her affection, and his adolescent urges for emancipation, all the more acutely felt because his mother now strongly insisted on his need for growing up. With a great sense of inferiority about his late effeminacy he set about proving to the world and to himself he could be more masculine than an ordinarily maturing youth, he could be, to use his own language, "a hard guy."

If space permitted, summaries of the case records might be given to set forth all of the emotional attitudes which were uncovered in these 19 delinquents whose family backgrounds did not seem to present special hazards for the upbringing of children. In at least 17 of the cases emotional factors which had been of great significance for the development of delinquency were revealed. The nature of these we have scheduled at the end of this chapter, together with the dynamic factors in the two other cases.

While we are considering this limited series of 19 delinquents, we may contrast the controls paired with them, even though the avoidance of delinquency on the part of the controls was hardly anything more than we might expect —certainly not such a noteworthy phenomenon as the nondelinquency of the controls who had inimical family backgrounds. And although in a later chapter we organize our entire material on differentiating emotional experiences, from this present series we can very well select some illustrative examples of contrast.

With 16 of these controls it came out very clearly that they were at least ordinarily happy young people who felt that they were well enough adjusted in their life situations; they were obtaining satisfactions and gave no evidence of suffering from internal conflicts. To be sure, none of them were neurotic or abnormal personalities, but what a contrast with the delinquents to find in such a large proportion no indication whatever of significant emotional disturbances! One illustration of such good adjustments—in this instance accomplished in spite of handicaps—may serve to emphasize

Favorable and Inimical Family Situations

the usually discoverable difference between the feeling life of controls and delinquents.

The control proved to be an undersized and underweight young fellow, twenty years old, with a deformed elbow and diseased teeth and tonsils. He was a decidedly poorer physical specimen than his delinquent brother of fourteen. His intelligence level was no higher, nor was he as talented as the brother who took considerable delight in his ability to draw. Nevertheless the control had achieved notable satisfactions all through his school life, as well as in working after school hours and more recently in steadily holding a job, in reading, music, and keeping company with a nice girl. He made no such complaints about the family life as did his brother, indeed he insisted that for him it had been fairly comfortable.

The delinquent was the youngest of the family. He had been a healthy, fat baby and an active young child, more vigorous than his older brother was at that age. He was nursed for sixteen months and then allowed to suck from the bottle until he was five years old. The control was nursed only six months and given no bottle. The control's childhood was unremarkable from the standpoint of behavior either at home or at school. Not so with the delinquent—even in his first school year he was regarded as a difficult problem. He was registered as an utterly spoiled boy, hard to discipline, always wanting his own way. When he was nine a competent school visitor worked for long on his problem; then at ten years he was studied at a clinic because he was showing many nervous habits and was subject to fears.

By the time we saw him at fourteen his delinquencies had been exceedingly numerous and some of them very serious—he confessed that they began when he was eight years old. Although he had been under arrest seven times, he and his family were able to tell of many offenses that were not on the court record. The boy's desire for traveling amounted almost to dromomania. During the last few years he had run away ten or more times, visiting most states of the Eastern seaboard.

The parents were hard-working immigrants, living in a decent neighborhood where the placid mother had a little shop in the front of the house that they owned. The father, high-strung, stubborn and rather frequently intoxicated, showed really great concern about the boy. During two years of partial unemployment this man gave much time to watching his son and attempting to manage him—this began when the latter was about eleven years old. Since he was nine or even earlier the boy had been treated harshly by the father, especially when the latter was drunk, and now when the father attempted so definitely to manage him there grew up terrific antagonism between them—the father growing more irritable and stubborn, the boy more moody and wilful. After some of the delinquent's escapades the older brother also took a hand in punishing him. The mother maintained a forgiving attitude, did not even scold the boy, but at the time when we studied the case was more or less rejective of him.

A curious phase of this boy's personality development was found in his attitude toward praise and punishment. Several of the school people said that he simply could not stand praise; when he received it, he at once became obstreperous. Yet on the other hand it was noted that whippings at home seemed to have precipitated further and more serious delinquencies. On one occasion the boy indulged in an orgy of stealing for two or three weeks just after he had been arrested and placed on probation. It seemed at times as though he courted punishment. Another time after some delinquency he gave himself up to a policeman. Once he stated that he would have to punish himself if nobody else did. He had many dreams of disaster befalling him, and often insisted, though with some contradictions, that he must be sent to a reform school. In court he avowed that something seemed to force him to do what he did.

In writing for us a short sketch of his life and of his ambitions he inscribed below one of his cartoons, "Little by little I have become to be what I am." Naturally one could but agree with this; his established patterns of behavior had long been in the making. The modification of these was clearly seen to involve alteration of his life situation, especially the father-son relationship, as well as prolonged psychiatric treatment for his neurotic character and personality. This was a program that was hardly under way before further delinquency led to his being committed to a correctional school. Now on parole at eighteen he evidently is comporting himself very much better.

In all the years of family turmoil the control sailed along complacently, feeling himself quite superior, probably enjoying his recognized status when he was allowed to administer punishment. To us he proclaimed that he was the serious and steady brother, adding "My parents never tried to run my life for me."

Of these 19 controls there were three, only three, from whom we could get any evidences of serious discontents. Let us shortly consider how it happened that their reactions to unhappiness did not take the form of delinquency, although they had a delinquent sibling.

One control, largely under the influence of a spoiling, interfering, domineering grandmother was much at outs with his parents for producing so many children—to his great disadvantage as an older brother. In aggressively expressing his discontents, he became a very disturbing influence in the family circle which otherwise was harmonious. His behavior was so explosive and reeked so much of suspicion and bitterness that at first he was thought possibly to be in the early stages of a psychosis. With sneers he avoided all his delinquent brother's associates and though "a devil at home" he worked well outside and kept free from unlawful behavior.

With another control perhaps we are overstepping the mark in intimating that he had anything like the heavy emotional load from which his delinquent brother suffered. Disgusted with his parents' old world standards and superstitions, this nondelinquent youth had been altogether unhappy in his home life. He reacted to his discontents by establishing a definite goal for himself—education became everything to him. He grew to be desperately selfish, unsympathetic with his parents who were really very decent people, and enormously proud of his achievement because he considered that he had lifted himself quite above the family level. As an aside it may be mentioned that the delinquent, the only one among eight children, was a far pleasanter personality and in spite of his having received much punishment at their hands was far more sympathetic with his parents.

The third control with discontents, a boy fifteen years old, though having nothing comparable to the unhappy situation of his delinquent brother, had long felt rejected because the mother and sister strongly favored this younger brother and his father preferred the sister. But fortunately for him he was a rough-and-tumble lad, thoroughly gregarious, much interested in athletics and somewhat in girls—all this being in great contrast to his brother's effeminate tendencies which he scorned. He found himself able through all this to meet and shoulder his emotional difficulties manfully. Then we discovered that the boy at least earlier had very strong religious convictions and had felt deeply sinful after once engaging in truancy with his brother and sharing in stolen spoils. His conscience sorely pricked him and this together with the fact that he was able to obtain other satisfactions helped him to refrain from further delinquencies.

The story of this family is worth sketching as demonstrating so clearly the variables that may exist for the development of emotional attitudes. The mother, an artistic and successful dressmaker, was displeased at her pregnancy with a third child, our case; but then she and her daughter, six years old, decided that they badly wanted a girl baby. After the advent of the child the mother seems to have allowed her desire for a girl to overbalance all good judgment. She proceeded to bring up the boy as much like a girl as possible, showering affection on him and using all her art to adorn him much and often in feminine array, being aided and abetted in this by her daughter. Until he was thirteen he was frequently elaborately costumed, even to go out on the street. The boy was also taught to sew and embroider.

The father played only a negative role in the family management. His version to us of the cause of his attitudes was that he himself had been domineered over and too strictly handled by his own father, so that he felt that his children should be entirely brought up by the mother.

Of course the boy through his feminine upbringing was isolated from other boys and hence grew unsocial, effeminate in mannerisms and appearance, and was affectionally too strongly attached to his mother. He entered a rather early puberty and then, through sensing his lack of normal masculinity, feeling thwarted, and being jealous of his extrovert brother, he became greatly discouraged and made some half-hearted attempts at emancipating himself by running away. At the time we saw him he had been engaged in much stealing for a year or more, principally from school. On his expeditions from home his effeminate appearance led homosexual men to be attracted to him and on several occasions he was easily led into their practices. Seeing him at thirteen years of age, we found a sensitive, discouraged boy apparently very amenable to suggestion. He, too, through his upbringing had a strong religious feeling about his sins and stated that he had half-hoped that he would be caught and punished.

We are able to add that through continued psychiatric aid which the family accepted very well the reconstruction of their attitudes, as well as of the boy's behavior has been highly satisfactory.

Those Living in Family Situations Apparently Inimical

MANY children living under conditions which seem to offer sufficient reason for the development of delinquent tendencies do not become delinquent. This is an outstanding fact not to be lost sight of when family situations are stressed, as they properly should be, as partial causes of delinquency. The point is that if some children are able to withstand a given inimical asocial environment, particularly as represented by the family life and its neighborhood setting, the environment considered by itself cannot logically be regarded as the only factor in the production of delinquency.

Even in many homes which for various reasons are considered thoroughly "bad," some children are non-delinquent.[1]

To be sure, the environmental situation, especially if we include in this term the family interrelationships, never is quite the same for any two children even in the same family. The complexity of what is properly to be considered environment comes to the fore particularly in our present studies of families. Above all we find extraordinary differences in the treatment of different children and in attitudes exhibited toward them—and certainly such data of family life are properly to be subsumed under the head of environmental situations which confront the child.

From our immensely interesting investigation of the causes for non-delinquency, we may summarize the life situations, physical conditions, personality characteristics, and special interests that lend themselves to first interpretations of why controls living under seemingly adverse circumstances were not delinquent. Since the situations were obviously inimical, there is no occasion at this point to examine the reasons for delinquency developing. Also we here refrain from taking into account differences in the feeling response—contentment as against discontent, happiness versus unhappiness—that have impressed us as so generally distinguishing delinquents from controls who lived under either favorable or inimical conditions. These important and more deeply revealing contrasts we leave for discussion in the next chapters.

1. While Clifford Shaw's notable studies of delinquency in compared sections of various cities (see, for example, his Chicago studies, *Delinquency Areas,* 1929) uncovered the fact that 23 per cent of the children in the worst sections appeared in the juvenile court, yet even this astounding figure leaves a great majority not registered as delinquents. Our intimate studies of families go a great deal further in offering challenging material for discussion. When we take our 111 families with inimical conditions for the upbringing of children, conditions which we have enumerated in our chapter on the entire series of families, we find that among 377 children of delinquent age there were 170 delinquents. So even these careful studies of the families show that 207 (55 per cent) of the children were non-delinquent.

Favorable and Inimical Family Situations

To be accounted for are 75 non-delinquents[2] coming from inimical circumstances, all of whom had at least one delinquent sibling. Why according to the more readily discernible categories of factors were these controls not delinquent?

Those with whom fortuitous circumstances largely accounted for escape from delinquency—the individual was somehow out of the picture, perhaps living elsewhere when the sibling developed his delinquent trends—6 controls.

Those so physically handicapped that it would have been difficult or even impossible for them to engage in the type of delinquency that the sibling entered into—7 controls.

Those with special interests to which they gave much time and energy—educational achievement, church activities, competitive athletics, work, etc.—11 controls.

Those who showed marked negative qualities that tended to keep them out of delinquency—being especially non-aggressive, introverted, shy, retiring, babyish, dependent, lacking in energy, etc.—10 controls.

Those who, though not showing marked negative qualities, were simply much quieter and less restless than their delinquent siblings. Demanding less from the environment, they were able to obtain sufficient satisfactions under their ordinary conditions of home life, in school, or from simple recreations—representing easily satisfied individuals—22 controls.

Those with positive personality characteristics and no apparent inferiority feelings who, notwithstanding lack of dominating interests, deliberately avoided delinquency through the establishment of ordinarily good, but very defi-

2. The figures for the controls living under inimical conditions vary from those for the delinquents because of marked differences sometimes found in attitudes taken by parents toward delinquents and controls—the control perhaps not having been met by harshness or not having experienced friction or disagreement about his upbringing. It appears that 11 more of the controls than of the delinquents lived in situations that seemed relatively favorable.

nite satisfactions in school life, social contacts, recreations, etc.—19 controls.

It was on just such a comparatively surface level of interpretation that the controls, many of them, vouchsafed an explanation of their escape from delinquency. Classification of a long list of their statements shows that their explanations vary greatly—centering on their ambitions, courage, companionship, religious tendencies, conscience, fears, or on their ability to reason, or even on the fact of a close tie to a mother.

In illustration are the following short transcripts selected from many similar remarks made by the controls:

"I want to make something of myself; I want to get an education."—"I wanted to get ahead in the world."

"I had courage to refuse to go with bad boys."—"I can lick anybody."—"In a bad crowd I can say no."—"My brother is a sissy and he goes with those fellows"—this was from one of the younger twins.—Another one of twins, older boys, said, "I played with the same boys, but they couldn't talk me over into crooking."

"It's the friends you make. I couldn't break away from good ones anymore than my brother could break away from bad ones."

"I want to be a priest."—"I want to be a missionary."

"I think it pays to be good."—"I used to grab things with the crowd when I was a little kid, eleven or twelve. Then I met a fellow up in the country; he was a hard worker; we used to talk over things in the evenings, but he wasn't preachy. Always he used to say, 'You never get anything for nothing; even a thief works hard but in a wrong way.' This turned me; what he said stuck by me."

"I just felt I couldn't disobey."—"I guess something inside me made me want to do right as I see it."

"I was always afraid to get in trouble."—"I was afraid of the cops."

"Well, I have been what you might call a mama's boy; I have stayed most of the time with her and haven't gone out for trouble"—this came from a husky boy, sixteen years of age.—And a prize fighter of twenty four, contrasting himself with his younger delinquent brother also made much of his attachment to his mother: "I was different when I was a boy, I would do anything for my mother. My home meant more to me than anything else. With my father just as good as on the ash heap it was up to me to look after her."

DATA RELATED TO FAMILY SITUATIONS

Living in apparently inimical situations				Living in apparently favorable situations			
Delinquents 86		Controls 75		Delinquents 19		Controls 30	
Personality deviates	Normal personality	Personality deviates	Normal personality	Personality deviates	Normal personality	Personality deviates	Normal personality
11	75	1	74	14	5	1	29

DELINQUENTS LIVING IN APPARENTLY FAVORABLE FAMILY SITUATIONS

A

Interpretations in Terms of Personality Factors

Physical or constitutional factors

Neurotic or psychoneurotic personality	5
Post-traumatic personality	2
Endocrine disorder, possibly complicated by earlier encephalitis	1
Endocrine disorder plus adolescent upset	1
Marked adolescent upset	3
Boy with peculiar feminine physique	1
Excessive prematurity	1

14 cases

Other factors in remainder
   Strong reactions to family restrictions   2
   Reactions to loneliness and boredom   2
   Obsessive pleasure in reckless automobile driving 1
                                                    —
                                                    5 cases
                                                    —
                                                    19 cases

B
Interpretations in Terms of Emotional Attitudes

Strong emotional attitudes discovered
   Strong feeling of being rejected by one or both parents   2
   Feelings of rejection plus inferiority   1
   Feelings of discouragement at not being understood by parents   2
   Feeling deprived as compared to brother   1
   Great antagonism between father and boy   1
   Very lonely through losing friend   1
   Severe mental conflicts plus feeling rejected   1
   Strong uncomplicated feelings of inadequacy or inferiority   4
   Feelings of inferiority plus:
      Feeling deprived of earlier spoiling   1
      Conflict about homosexual tendencies   1
      Marked adolescent upset and conflicts   1
      Conflict about mother fixation   1
                                                             —
                                                             17 cases

No strong emotional attitudes discovered
   Likable, very active boy with quite insufficient outlets mainly on account of economic stress in family, also because of father's old-world restrictive standards; much involved with very delinquent companion; acknowledged much influence by gangster pictures. Feels thwarted in normal desires and punished too much by father; jealous

of brothers—but only mild emotional reactions discovered   1
Spoiled boy with remarkably ingratiating personality and excessive prematurity who early discovered that he could with ease obtain pleasurable returns through misrepresentations and professionally conceived larcenies   1
                                                                                   ──
                                                                                   2 cases
                                                                                   ──
                                                                                   19 cases

CHAPTER VII

THE TWINS
DELINQUENTS AND CONTROLS

THE study of differences in the behavior tendencies of twins is of profound interest because, certain variables being automatically eliminated, better evaluations can be made of the causes of differences. When twins are compared we need not be concerned—as we have to be when studying siblings who are not twins—with age differences, with influences of the physical environment which may not be the same for children of different ages, with differences in ordinal position of the children in the family, with differences in parental attitudes at various periods due to health conditions, age changes, and so on. For all these and for many other aspects of the life situation the data are the same for twins who have been brought up together.

The good fortune of having eight pairs of twins in our series of delinquents and controls leads us more readily than in our other sibling comparisons to come to some clearer definition of the factors which tend to produce or prevent delinquency. These twins, all non-identical or dizygotic, and all boys except one girl control, ranged from six to seventeen years of age—only two pairs, however, being under twelve. Even the six-year-old was well started in delinquency and five of the others were heavy offenders. Here again we may well speak of the controls' escape from delinquency because six of these pairs of twins lived under conditions which we have considered decidedly inimical for the proper upbringing of a child.

Hoping through our studies of twins to find some combinations or to produce some spot-patterns which would characterize delinquents and not controls and which would enable us to state definitely that such-and-such an association of factors almost inevitably spells delinquency, we charted all the factors which according to observation or theory are considered genetically related to delinquency.[1] But save for the combination of abnormal personality plus deeply felt thwartings and dissatisfactions plus inimical family conditions, a combination which is applicable to only a few cases, we have not been able to discover any semblance to such a clear-cut composite of factors which prognosticate delinquency. Even this combination we know does not lead to an inevitable result; it may be remembered that in our main series there is a control with all these factors who avoided delinquency by

[1]. Johannes Lange's picturesque presentation of his studies of twins has received so much attention from students of delinquency—particularly because of its recommendation by J. B. S. Haldane—that it seems worth while for us here to comment on it. *Verbrechen als Schicksal,* or as published in English, *Crime and Destiny,* compares the careers of twins, identical and non-identical, and the title tells the story. While acknowledging the importance of this kind of investigation and the value of much material produced by Lange, we, with other commentators, are inclined to be highly critical of his conclusions and to regret the inadequacy of his material. Perhaps the main point for mention here is that his series of 13 identical twins upon which he bases the conception that criminality is fate represents almost entirely cases of abnormal personality, such as we place in one special category because of the peculiar likelihood of their becoming delinquent. And of course, if one of identical twins is abnormal upon a presumably organic basis we should certainly expect the other to be likewise. So the argument is almost an instance of begging the question.

No case of identical twins appears in the present research material, but once we had a most striking example. A delinquent boy seen by us was readily diagnosable as an abnormal personality of the ego-centric unstable type. While under observation it was accidentally discovered that he had a twin brother, evidently an identical twin of whom he had never heard and from whom he had been separated earlier than one year of age. We naturally expected to find that the brother was also an abnormal personality, and it proved that he had already been so diagnosed elsewhere. Nor were we at all surprised to hear that he was in a correctional institution. The similar behavior of these boys was not due to the fact that they were identical twins, but rather to both being abnormal personalities of the type that is particularly prone to show delinquent trends. If they had not been twins or even brothers and both were abnormal in the above sense, we should have thought the chance of their both being delinquent was very great.

spending a great deal of his time unhealthily in phantasy. Although not delinquent he of course presented a problem of mental hygiene.

If we take for these twins any single item or grouping of items from the factual material which seems in these or other cases to bear upon the development of delinquent trends, we are left with no picture of genetic factors that presents a high degree of probable validity—with one great exception, an exception that holds true for all in this smaller series of cases—the fact of deeply felt emotional discomfort. For example, as possibly betokening a conditioning of the personality that would eventuate in delinquency we have considered much crying and nervous manifestations in infancy and early childhood, versus quietude of the control. Now four delinquents did show an excess of such manifestations as against the quietness of the twin, but four did not, and indeed the control twin in one instance was the crying fussy baby. With regard to early and continued overrestlessness, the findings are a little stronger—four of the delinquent twins were exceedingly active or uninhibited and four were not, while all of the controls were either normally quiet or normally inhibited, one being an unusually subdued youngster. All other differences, such as weight at birth, variations in the nursing experience, in severe or many illnesses, in biological or mental equipment, or in personality characteristics show up even less strongly.

This brings us to consideration of the above mentioned exception, namely, strongly-felt emotional disturbance; here we have an entirely different story. Assembling the records of these twins we find a one-to-one correlation between affective discomforts and the onset or the continuance of delinquency. Every one of the delinquents proved to have these inner stresses and every one of the controls proved to be free from them.

Short narratives which tell the family situations, the reciprocal relationships of parents and children, and which reveal the conditioning experiences and reactive tendencies of delinquents and controls will serve to show how basic and far-reaching all these may be for the production or prevention of delinquency. These sketches at the same time offer illustrations of most of the sources of emotional disturbance, the discussion of which will be the subject of the next chapter.

A

WE may begin with our six-year-old twins. Although so young the delinquent had already definitely. run away twice and on numerous occasions had wandered from home, having been picked up by the police several times. On one occasion he made a serious attempt to set the house on fire. He was a truant from school and had repeatedly stolen, even considerable amounts, from teachers as well as from his parents. He had also stolen money from a neighbor's apartment, a hospital, and a gasolene station. Moreover, his parents complained of his disobedience, impudence to his mother and his temper tantrums. In general he was regarded as being extremely troublesome at school and incorrigible at home. The control was an even tempered, obedient, thoroughly well behaved "model child."

The twins in this family of three children were the result of a welcomed pregnancy; the control was born first and without instruments, the delinquent was delivered by instruments during a difficult labor. They weighed about six pounds each; they were both bottle fed from the time of birth. The delinquent was a fussy crying baby; the control was not. They both had an uneventful health history and were of about equal size and in good physical condition at the time of our study; they both exhibited occasional enuresis, but neither had any nervous habits. Our psychologist gave the delinquent an intelligence rating of I.Q. 82, commenting that probably he would have done considerably better if his attention could have been fully held. The I.Q. of the control was 95. The summing up of the personality characteristics of the delinquent shows that he was exceedingly restless, active, impulsive, uninhibited, continually running off to play with other boys, among whom he was regarded as a follower. He frequently acted as a "show off," being specially delighted with the attention he received because he was such a small boy when he was held in the detention home for a few days, and he was especially proud of his grinning picture in the newspapers which had appeared once after he had been found by the police. At home he was said to be extraordinarily inquisitive, "into everything." In the physical examination he appeared to have some shame about his body.

The control was an amenable, pleasant youngster, much quieter, self-reliant and easily amused at home, preferring to be with his mother rather than to play with other boys, although he did sometimes go out to play.

The family lived in crowded quarters, but there was no great financial stress. Earlier they had lived in better homes and in decent neighborhoods, though they moved much because the father frequently sold the home. The parents were thoroughly incompatible, engaged in much open quarreling and often, even before the children, made counter accusations and threatened divorce. There was violent disagreement about discipline; the mother charged her high-tempered husband with whipping too severely and he maintained that although she was rather well educated she was really dull; incompetent and too lenient.

An amazing difference of attitude on the part of the father toward the delinquent and the control was reported to us and acknowledged by him. He maintained that the cause of it was the stubborn lack of response to him shown by the delinquent when an infant, only two months old. He said he detested the boy then and had ever since—"I can't bear to have him touch me. I would rather have a snake around me than have him." Though the mother stated that the father always repulsed the boy when the latter attempted to climb on his knee, both parents insisted that the child had never given expression to any strong feelings about being disliked by his father.

The older boy of eight had been very jealous of the twins from the time of their birth and cruel to them. He suffered from epileptic attacks for two years and afterward simulated attacks in order to gain attention. Though particularly hating our delinquent, or perhaps because of this hatred, he entered into delinquencies with him and inducted him into sex practices. As the result of frequent beatings and the family disturbances, this older boy had emotional tensions of his own and, besides, gave evidences of being an epileptic personality.

Both the delinquent and the control had plenty of toys and at times had a playroom to themselves. They both went to Sunday School fairly regularly and willingly.

The delinquent freely unburdened himself to the psychiatrist, telling many of his delinquencies, some of which were not known. About stealing a considerable sum from his teacher he said rather demurely that his Dad had to pay it back. In childish fashion he told of "other kids" inciting him to set the house on fire. His story included "another boy" with a name similar to his own, "a bad boy"—"He was mad at my Dad and set the house on fire. Then I was afraid and we got the fire mostly out by stepping on the curtains before the firemen came." He went on to give in the plainest language the vile epithets which his father called him and also the equally opprobrious terms that his parents applied to each other. He showed much feeling about all this, saying that he was going to hit his father "right on the chin" some day. He also evinced great dislike of his older brother and shame about their sex play together. The control, he said, never did such things. It came out very clearly that the boy felt extremely insecure in his family relationships and that he greatly craved recognition and affection.

The control, on the contrary, was very sure of himself and quite well satisfied with things as they were. In speaking of his brother to the psychologist he priggishly boasted, "I am the good boy."

THE sources of emotional disturbance are clear: the delinquent deeply sensed the deprivation of his father's love, indeed plainly verbalized his knowledge of being hatefully rejected and his own antagonism to his father. He also felt greatly discriminated against and exceedingly jealous of both his siblings, craving to be on an equal affectional and recognitional footing with them. About the family disharmonies there were intense discomforts and he also had considerable sense of guilt on account of mutual masturbatory practices with the older brother.

The reactive behavior is readily interpreted and includes attempt at escape from unpleasant situations, attempt at revenge, and attempt to get substitutive satisfactions. The last is shown by his enjoyment of gaining recognition even as a delinquent—his wounded ego was bolstered up by obtaining status in competition with his older brother who in spite of being also severely delinquent had experienced much more affection and recognition. School incorrigibility was evidently a carry-over of rebellion against hated authority.

Our long years of experience lead us to see in this case the emotional backgrounds from which, unless sharply modified, a delinquent and criminal career is very likely to emerge.

B

ONE of twins, 13 years old, was heavily delinquent especially with a companion; he had broken into several places and stolen and engaged in other larcenies for which he had been in court and in a detention home twice when we saw him. The control had never been delinquent.

The father had been dead for two years; earlier he had been away for long periods in a tuberculosis sanitarium. The rather dull mother was, for reasons that became obvious, much on the defensive and though frequently seen it was impossible to get from her a detailed account of the development of these twins, the youngest of five children. However it does appear probably true that there was little difference between their size and condition at birth and that the nursing period of three or four months and their health histories had been much the same. As an infant the delinquent cried much more than his twin. His mother said that she didn't bother about him and thought that her husband, who was evidently a kindly man, spoiled him by picking him up so much.

As we studied them, the twins showed close similarities and marked differences. They were of the same height, being 4½ inches below the age-norm, both appeared healthy with rather attractive features, but the delinquent was ten pounds heavier and was a greater eater, while the control was fussy about food. The delinquent was enuretic and a severe nail-biter, the control had neither of these habits. Their I.Q.'s were 71 and 75 respectively. They were both in the seventh grade, our case being now in the public and the control in the parochial school. They both had attended the latter school, but the delinquent had been expelled on account of bad conduct. He still was known as a restless inattentive pupil and was on probation in his grade. The control was an amenable hard worker and because of his promotions had little insight into his limitations—he talked of going to college.

There was a great contrast in their personality characteristics. The delinquent was immensely active, never content to sit still or stay at home; outside the home he appeared a merry friendly extrovert, dirty and untidy, full of zest for play and adventure. The control was much less active, timid in company, shy, preferring to be alone or to help his mother in household work. He was courteous, serious, neat, tidy, and affectionate to his mother.

The home was in a very poor neighborhood; the family had received charitable aid for years and agency visitors found the mother unwilling to raise her standards; indeed there were unconfirmed rumors of drinking men visiting in the household.

The behavior of the delinquent when at home was utterly different from that of the control. He was aggressively noisy, spiteful, teasing, inquisitive about his mother's affairs, and took every occasion to torment her. She said herself that he had often threatened to call in the police—"He even threatens to call the cops when I go out for a walk at night."

The boy's most recalcitrant and delinquent behavior began when he was associating with a boy who was notorious in school for his sexual propensities. From him the delinquent derived much sexual ideation. Then with another much brighter boy, also one of our delinquents, who came from a family where there was much bickering and where the drinking father openly before the children accused the mother of illicit sex affairs, he became involved in serious delinquency. Together these boys concocted an accusatory obscene letter and tacked it on the door or the gate of a woman in their neighborhood. The projection of their own ideas concerning their own mothers is obvious.

The control, largely through his contentment at home, never mixed with his brother's companions, never developed his brother's unfortunate sex ideation, and so did not question his mother's behavior. He thus avoided emotional tensions.

We found the delinquent beneath his often merry exterior a really heart-sick boy with strong emotional disturbances centering about a feeling of being rejected by his mother, whereas his brother was favored. Jealousy ensued and he had deep feelings, which he could never completely unburden to us, about his suspicions of his mother's conduct.

His reactive behavior took the form of unconscious or at least unverbalized desire to punish his mother by making life difficult for her, and perhaps also the exhibition of anti-social attitudes was for him a getting even with the world, while the thrills of reckless delinquent adventure somehow represented the attempt to obtain substitutive gratifications. If it had been possible to dig further into his feeling-life, unquestionably other elements in his dissatisfactions would have been found but the above is enough to explain his overt misbehavior.

C

Biologists know the mechanism by which it is possible for one of twins, as in the following instance, to have heredity quite different from the other.

These twins were sixteen years old when we studied them, having appeared about midway among fifteen pregnancies, with ten of the children surviving. Their ignorant mother insists that she had a perfectly healthy pregnancy, that their birth was easy, and that they were just alike when they were born. The delinquent cried much during infancy and was nursed only two months, while the control was a very placid child and was nursed for a year. The health history of the delinquent is largely negative although earlier he complained of severe headaches. The control suffered from many illnesses, especially throat and ear ailments, having had two mastoid operations.

When we saw them the twins were of exactly the same height, being 5 inches below the age-norm. The delinquent was enormously strong, with big bones and muscles, large features, piercing eyes, and at times a very hard or "tough" expression. His tonsils and teeth were in bad condition; he showed marked coarse tremors of the hands. The control was of normal nutrition, but more lightly built, with rather sensitive features and a quiet expression. His hearing was somewhat defective. The delinquent performed school achievements tests on about a sixth grade level, I.Q. 85; the control had reached seventh grade, I.Q. 76. Both were working boys.

The delinquent had been in court several times, mainly for assault and battery, but also earlier for truancy. Many complaints of his unruliness, even to the extent of fighting a teacher, had been made by the school authorities. As a younger boy he frequently slept out anywhere away from home. More recently he had belonged to a gambling crowd.

In personality characteristics the delinquent had been an extremely active, restless, crowd-boy with a violent temper and rough manners. Since a little boy he had proclaimed that he always got the worst of it, and vindictively attacked anybody. When he had a job, he was a very hard worker, preferring the roughest labor, but often quarreled with employers. He appeared somewhat hypomanic. The control was normally energetic and even tempered; he never went with a crowd, worked quietly and steadily at his jobs, and was notably pleasant spoken.

The parents were Italian immigrants. The father a psychotic, diagnosed manic-depressive, with strong persecutory ideas at times, earned fairly well at periods. He ruled over his children with an iron hand when they were young. Two years before the twins were born he was committed for the first time as insane and up to the time of our study had been alternately paroled and recommitted some ten times. During these years he had produced seven children!! The illiterate mother was a thrifty neat housekeeper, though the home was so crowded that four boys slept in one bed. She was found to be stubborn and forever complaining about America and its institutions to the workers of the many social agencies where she applied for aid.

The delinquent voiced to us his long unhappiness, saying that as far back as he could remember he was hated by his whole family. None had any use for him and his father's favorite was his twin brother; the latter always was given better clothes and some money to spend. "I was told to be good like he is. And look at him, he is a sheik and goes out with girls. I don't care how I look." He detested his father. When there was quarreling at home, he used to run out and sleep anywhere. He made many accusations of being "picked on" by teachers and employers and said he hadn't any good friends in the world.

The control expressed moderate satisfaction with both home and school life, saying, "I have been treated all right."

THE delinquent strongly felt rejections, insecurities, discomforts about family disharmonies, hatreds, jealousies and inferiorities—all these tensions added to the inherited instabilities of an abnormal or possibly prepsychotic personality. As a matter of fact this boy, as far as we could learn, resembled his father in behavior tendencies more than any of the other children, and probably this was the reason for the great clash between them.

The reactive patterns were those of flight and attempt to win compensations for inferiority by aggressive hostilities in which he was able to bolster up his ego through his physical prowess.

D

A STILL more striking example of contrast in constitutional equipment, at least of congenital if not of hereditary origin, as well as of emotional backgrounds was found in twins, a boy and a girl, seventeen years of age, living near New Haven. The boy was rather short and plump, with round face and soft, fair skin. He was immaculately dressed, had plucked eyebrows, and even at the clinic took out a pocket mirror and tried to improve his complexion. On physical examination he was found to have a supernumerary mammary nipple on one side but no apparent anomalies of the sex organs; with his rounded contours, his rouged cheeks and exaggerated feminine mannerisms there was no mistaking the type. The girl was of average height, slenderly built with small breasts, narrow hips, and shoulders relatively broad for a girl. She appeared to be an unaffected healthy-minded, normal adolescent.

There were three children in the family, one older brother having been born ten years before the twins. The mother stated that for nine years she had wanted a girl baby and was happy at being pregnant again. It was a sickly pregnancy and much care had to be taken to prevent a miscarriage; however it was a full-time delivery, the boy weighing $4\frac{1}{2}$ and the girl $3\frac{1}{2}$ pounds. The babies were put on the bottle at once and through skillful feeding neither showed any nutritional difficulty. The boy was a particularly good baby, big, fat and healthy, and he remained in good health all during his childhood. After one year of age the girl required a great deal of attention; she cried a great deal and had spells of holding her breath. During her childhood she had some severe illnesses. The boy was right-handed, but she was left-handed and had been trained to use her right hand. Until she was thirteen she had some nervous habits of biting her nails or picking at a paper, habits which the boy never had.

Until they were four or five, the twins were dressed rather similarly; the boy always wanted to have clothes of the same color and material as his sister and to wear her beads and other ornaments. The control played normally with her girl friends, but the boy was afraid of other boys and played with dolls and at other games with his sister's friends. They went to the same school and demonstrated good abilities (our study shows I.Q. 107 for the boy, for the girl 113), but the boy grew lazy and failed in the tenth grade while the girl continued on in school, making a good record. In later boyhood the delinquent did not have much companionship and would enter very little into boyish sports although he was not seclusive. Boys classified him as snobbish and he preferred to be with adults. The control liked to play active games, had many girl friends, belonged to the scouts, and as she advanced in years began to take an interest in boys. She had the reputation everywhere of being a conscientious, fine normal girl. To us she expressed much disgust with her brother's tendencies and delinquencies.

The delinquent was referred to us because as a young homosexual he had been soliciting men in a park, but we found there was much more than that to the story of his delinquencies. At ten years of age he began truancy, staying out over night in parked cars and running away from home. At that age he was first in the juvenile court and not a few times later was apprehended by the police and placed in detention homes. In the last two years he had gone on trips to distant cities, once reaching Hollywood. His parents would be communicated with by the police and would send funds for his return. At ten years of age he once stole $10 when he ran away and also took money with which to go to shows. He frequently purloined silk underclothes from his mother and sister. More recently he had taken a considerable amount of money on several occasions but had never been known to have stolen except from his family.

This boy's homosexual activities began at the age of twelve and he gradually became more and more immersed in such affairs, so that by the time he was sixteen when away from home he lived with men for immoral purposes and received money from them. At times he paraded on the street in girl's clothes.

We found an indolent boy, unsocial except with his own type of companions. He had many body interests, said he was proud of his "shape," and liked to be well dressed. He was a great reader, particularly of mystery stories, was extremely fond of the movies and theatres, and hoped himself to appear on the stage. Through correspondence and contacts he accumulated quite a collection of pictures and autographs of actors and actresses. He was typically conversational and argumentative, conceited and selfish. Toward his parents he was aggressively defiant and impudent; in apparently taking pains to annoy them he exhibited a vindictive and almost cruel attitude. With us he avowed that he had no intention whatever of relinquishing his homosexual life; the men with whom he consorted were of superior type; many celebrated men were homosexuals; indeed he intended to become a member of a colony of inverts.

The parents were an intelligent and companionable couple who until recently had lived in a good neighborhood under comfortable conditions with many advantages for the children. Not only the mother but also the father had expressed disappointment when it was announced that there was a boy as well as a girl born; however, although he often expressed partiality for his little girl he gave the boy much attention until the latter became defiant at about ten years of age. There was little doubt but that both parents spoke the truth when they said that they had tried to show equal affection for the two children. The twins when young attracted much attention and, on the whole, the parents were rather proud of them.

When the boy began to be delinquent, the father administered corporal punishment, but soon found that it did no good. With us the mother at first attributed even the boy's early misbehavior to his having been influenced by the movies. Questioned further she said that her older son had turned out so well that she greatly desired this boy to do likewise. She wanted him to "look nice" and thought it much better for him when little to play with "nice little girls" rather than with "bad boys." Later she had tried to persuade him to play with boys, but he could not get on with them. In the record of the boy when he appeared before the court at ten years of age, we read that the mother said then that he had played so much with girls that boys did not like him—evidently giving this in explanation of his truancy and running away.

The same record stated that this young boy, coming from an unusually good home, spoke up in court, critical and defiant of his parents, vehemently insisting that he did not want to go back home because he did not want to go to school. He even suggested a preferred alternative, asking the judge to send him to a correctional school. To us, the boy now seventeen appeared thoroughly nonchalant. He stated that it was not his fault that he was born or brought up that way. His mother had never given him any opportunity for playing with boys; he always had to play with his sister. He had never even played baseball.

The causes of this boy's homosexual tendencies need hardly concern us much here; unconscious dynamic psychological processes were undoubtedly factors, but the problem of genetics in such cases involves a complex of elements. Our main interest is in the various other delinquencies for which he earlier had been several times apprehended. Already at ten years the boy had evinced his emotional discomforts. He had an immense feeling of inadequacy in his relationship with boys when he had to meet them, as in school, and undoubtedly keenly realized his inferiority when they turned away from him. It seems that he could hardly then have felt himself rejected or deprived in his affectional family relationships, although we are not sure on this point because he may have sensed partiality for his sister. But he did at ten years and later feel that he had not been understood, had been mismanaged, and so had been greatly thwarted in normal masculine development. Because of this he hated his parents. About his first homosexual experiences at twelve it seems inevitable that he must have had much mental conflict proved by concealment then and later of such experiences.

His reactive behavior shows his ambivalences—he wanted to be a girl but, this being impossible and his ego being wounded by discovery of his social inadequacies as a male, he attempted to prove himself a real boy by being a successful runaway and by defiance of his parents. (This running away from good home circumstances and normally affectionate parents was all the more remarkable because it was on the part of an effeminate boy so largely unable to meet the world.) Of course the escape impulse was also active and attempt at revenge is shown clearly by repeated stealing from his parents and his openly vindictive behavior toward them. His later attempt to resolve the conflict was by the method of giving way to instinctual urges—the boy stated to us that from the first he thoroughly enjoyed all his homosexual practices.

E

OUR eight-year-old twins presented a picture of contrasts, that, except for its appearance in twins, is very familiar to us. The intelligent family and a skillful visiting teacher had come to quite a fair understanding of the situation before we entered upon our study. It remained only for some better insights to be gained and certain attitudes to be changed before great improvements were shown.

Life in a pleasant residential suburb of Boston offered many advantages for the children. They went to a public school where great interest was taken in personality development as well as in academic achievement. It was a family of culture; the well-educated mother was much, she acknowledged "too much," interested in activities outside the home; the father was a typically intense successful business man, taking his recreation in equally ardent devotion to sports. There were four older children who figured much in the family circle. In their perplexities about the delinquent the mother and a sister of twenty were especially coöperative with us and the school people.

The twins came four years after a previous pregnancy. The mother who did not know that she was carrying twins had a miserable time during pregnancy. She told us the boy who later became the delinquent was almost in her throat stifling her, but how she knew which twin it was we cannot surmise. Anyhow she was shocked to find that she had to go through a second labor; the future delinquent was born last and because his head was large had to be delivered by instruments. The twins were of about the same size at birth, were nursed six weeks and were both good, quiet babies. Their health histories were very similar; neither had suffered from any serious illness. The mother was in poor health for a couple of years after the twins came; she had to have several operations and so they received little attention from her. For their first four years they were brought up by a competent nurse who treated them fairly.

The twins presented marked physical differences when we studied them. Both were tall, the delinquent being 6 inches above the age-norm, and the control 4 inches. The former was of a delicate, distinctly asthenic build; the latter was particularly well-nourished, sturdy, and strong. They also contrasted greatly in coloring. The delinquent showed slight facial mannerisms and during the physical examination spoke of various bodily complaints; the control was boastful of his physical prowess.

The delinquent was generally known as an awkward clumsy inactive dreamy boy who was "out of it when other boys came to play with his brother." He sought affection and craved the recognition of adults; toward his father he seemed shy. He was sensitive to the extent that he became nauseated when reprimanded in school, and showed timidity or cowardliness, as his family called it, in many ways. Generally passive and amenable, he sometimes became excited in the company of other children and "acted up to gain attention." He was extraordinarily neat and orderly, showing aesthetic appreciation in making collections of various things. "He likes poetry and is the only one in the family who is imaginative."

It is enough to say of the control that he was a rough-and-tumble, care-free, untidy boy, thoroughly extroverted, able to approach his father and mix well with other boys.

In school the delinquent had at first done better work than his brother, but latterly much worse. His family considered him duller because he was so much slower in learning to play games of any kind. The visiting teacher, however, from her observation of the boy was not surprised to find that his I.Q. was 114 as compared to the control's 103.

The delinquency had been going on for two years. The mother reported that the boy had often pilfered little moneys and had taken small articles from an older brother and hidden them, then lying about it, much to the annoyance of the family. In school he had sometimes "borrowed," as the teacher euphoniously put it, crayons, clips, etc., from other pupils and the teacher. To us he confessed that he had repeatedly taken money from his father's pockets that no one had known about, and the control gave an instance of his brother's stealing fifty cents and treating boys with it.

The family with their ideals of honesty and truthfulness were much concerned about the delinquent. The control had always been so frank and honest that it was a great question with them why there should be so much difference between the twins. If the mother had ever been partial to the control, it was not revealed to us, but certainly nowadays she felt that the delinquent was a very queer youngster. The older girl, on the other hand, had always been very fond of the delinquent because she admired his aesthetic sensibilities and powers of imagination. The father had not much time to give to the twins, but it was clear that while he expressed no disgust with the boy, the delinquent was not the kind of a son he wanted. With the control the father freely engaged in rough play.

The older brother thought the delinquent "a weakling" and "a pest" and often in temper derided him for his cowardliness, his stealing, and lying.

The control with us expressed a distinct feeling of superiority; everything went well for him; at home and at school his interests were all in games and he hated to study. He stated he liked his father best of anyone in the family and in writing his name said, "I am Junior." Then he added, "I can lick anybody, my brother's just a sissy."

In interviews with the delinquent he frankly acknowledged that he was unhappy. For one thing he didn't like being a twin. "My brother is Junior." He definitely felt that he liked his mother better than his father and that he wanted more of her attention than he had been able to get. He was sure that his father preferred the control because the latter was more adept in activities. The attempt to get him to phrase other sources of unhappiness brought out that he had fears from which the control did not suffer, and that he hated school—"I am dumb." He said he had only one boy friend and that even this boy really liked the control better. When asked if he could not do anything especially well, he could think of nothing except that his handwriting was the best in his grade. When with his brother it was noted that he was very self-deprecatory. He evidently desired the control's approval; for example, he said that he didn't like the latter to see him studying—the connotation being that the control thought that real boys didn't study at home. He never once mentioned his older brother who disliked him, but did speak of the sister who gave him attention.

THE sources, then, of the boy's unhappiness were self-evident. He felt rejected by his father, somewhat affectionally insecure with his mother; he deeply sensed both real and fancied inadequacies; and undoubtedly was disturbed by his older brother's derision. Then there was strong sibling jealousy toward his twin with whom he was compared unfavorably.

His overt delinquent behavior represented attempts to get substitutive satisfactions, as when he spent his pilferings for sweets, etc., or went to the movies while his brother was enjoying active play. If he couldn't get the love and recognition he desired, then he would seize other pleasures. The revenge motive is plain in his repeated purloining of his older brother's possessions. Sometimes he attempted to get status that he couldn't otherwise obtain by buying the favor of other boys.

F

UNTIL a couple of months before we saw him, one of twelve-year-old twins had been delinquent for about two years and had been in court three times and in a detention home as often. The full story of his delinquencies did not come out till he related them to us. He began with companions to steal from the five-and-ten cent stores, then from other shops. They broke into several places and stole baseball supplies and money. Once the boy took $15 from his father with which to play gambling machines with these companions.

The complete family history was not obtainable because the mother had died two years earlier—a rather intelligent, hard-working immigrant, we were told—but the father was very anxious about the boy and though the latter had not been just recently delinquent his father was eager to understand the causes of the earlier delinquency and to prevent them in the future. There were ten children, all alive; the twins were the result of the seventh pregnancy. The pregnancy was healthy and the birth normal, the control being born first. The twins were of about the same size at birth, and were both nursed for about a year. They both "cried terribly" until they began to walk. In walking and talking the delinquent was always first; the father said that throughout childhood he seemed to be ahead in everything. All his life he has seemed to have more energy than the control. As a young child he would run away from the house and the control would stay inside. They both had the ordinary diseases of childhood mildly and some accidents of no special importance. The control stopped being enuretic when very young, the delinquent has continued in occasional bed-wetting. The father spoke of the very likable qualities of the delinquent boy and the stepmother who has been in the household for six months corroborated this. Both the twins were fond of sports, they had somewhat the same companions, but the father said of the control, "Somehow nobody leads him into trouble." The father emphasized the control's quietness and the fact that he would not be seen with some of the "wild boys" with whom his brother associated. They both read the same books and magazines and had always been good friends.

The twins though not looking at all alike proved to be closely similar in size and build, both being strong and healthy. We saw them in the autumn at which time they were attending the same school, the control half a grade ahead of his brother. For some reason the delinquent had been going for two previous years to another school not attended by his brother and there had failed in the sixth grade, but had partly made up his deficiency by attending summer school. Recently he had been given special school honors by being elected president of his class, as his brother had earlier been, and now was doing especially good work and keeping free from delinquency. In the former school he was rated as "incorrigible with capacity for leadership." The school record of the control mentions his reliable steady-going qualities. The I.Q. of the delinquent was 98; that of the control, 106.

Comparing personality characteristics, we found that the delinquent was much more active, energetic and restless, fond of fighting and wandering about, and less contented to stay at home than his brother. The latter was signalized by his modest, serious, and dignified behavior, but was said by his father to be less affectionate than the delinquent.

With us the delinquent boy frankly discussed his offenses and stated that the trouble all began with his great hatred of going to the school which was distant and out of his district, and with his special dislike of one teacher. Somehow then he turned to a "bad bunch of fellows" for companionship. Now he had broken away from them, partly because his older brother had engaged in sports with him during the summer and partly because he was having a good time in the present school. He always felt well adjusted in his family life and got along well with his stepmother. He hoped to be an amateur prize fighter as the older brother had been.

About all we could get from the control was to the effect that he had been satisfied with things as they were and that he picked out good companions to play with—"Anyhow nobody could talk me into going wrong."

Though they had been apparently overlooked by the school people the emotional sources of the delinquency in this case could have been easily found. A particularly active energetic boy had felt himself thwarted in normal impulses and desires and strongly sensed that he was discriminated against. He reacted violently by trying to get substitutive compensatory satisfactions which included the thrill of delinquent adventure. Lacking school status, he enjoyed recognition as a very active member of a delinquent crowd; undoubtedly also there was an unconscious revenge motive in his hostilities exhibited toward school authority.

G

One of twins, fifteen years old, had been in numerous and very serious delinquencies over a period of two years. He had been truant much and with companions had engaged in many burglaries. The police record gives a series of four burglaries in one night; besides this there had been much gambling and the boy had once escaped from a detention home and twice from a correctional school.

The control confessed to us that once when he was about twelve years old he started to rob a grocery store with two other fellows, but somebody came and frustrated the attempt. There seems to be no question of his having been in any other delinquency.

The parents of these boys were illiterate immigrants. The father was a steady-working gardener who had accumulated enough to own his cottage which was situated in a suburb of immigrants where there were "speak-easies," two houses of prostitution, and much law breaking. The mother had been a very robust peasant who worked in truck gardens and kept her home beautifully clean. She had been dead for two years when we studied the twins. There were seven older children alive; another set of twins had died earlier. Two of the older boys were definitely criminalistic and both had been in penal institutions; however it is only fair to say that these brothers had tried to keep the delinquent away from their gangs.

Our information about the family came from the sisters who were eager to coöperate. The pregnancy was healthy, delivery was normal; the control was born first. The mother had cried bitterly when the second baby came, saying that she had wanted no more children and here she had two. From the start our delinquent was more aggressive and vigorous; he aggressively seized the breast, got the milk, and the control had to be satisfied with the bottle. Though the delinquent never appeared to be sick, "he cried from the time he was born," whereas the control was normally placid. During all of his childhood the delinquent was never severely ill, but from babyhood he was exceedingly "nervous and restless." He always wanted to be roaming and would run away from the house when he was only two years old. The control had many colds and earaches. He was never restless and was always satisfied to remain at home. The control regularly slept with the mother until he was five; the delinquent slept with a sister. The delinquent was fussy about food, had a great craving for sweets, and showed much more sleep disturbance than the control who was satisfied with the family diet and slept quietly.

We found the delinquent to be a healthy-looking boy of normal height and development with rather a round full face, suggesting in general build the pyknic habitus. The control was very short, five inches below the age-norm but of normal weight for his height. He had many carious teeth and was somewhat defective in hearing.

Each of the boys had to repeat some classes; with barely passing marks they had only reached the seventh grade. The delinquent gained an I.Q. of about 80; the control, 78. The school record speaks of the restlessness, distractibility, and "emotional instability" of the delinquent, and the quiet "stability" of the control.

The sisters gave a clear account of the close relationship that had existed between his mother and the control; he followed her about and did household tasks with her. Generally the delinquent was not in the house long enough to do anything. As they grew older the control was very confidential with the mother and after she died was chummy with his sisters. The delinquent was always reticent with his family and sometimes sat about as if he had something on his mind. The father, a very restless man, "crabby and grouchy," seemed to dislike the delinquent from his early years; the sisters stated that this probably was because the boy was so much like himself. He always preferred the control who was of smiling and placid disposition, much like the mother in this respect.

The father frequently whipped the delinquent as he had done some of his other children but was much more tender with the control. It was the sisters' opinion that though the delinquent was not nearly so demonstrative and cried little after his mother's death, in reality he felt her loss even more keenly than did his twin.

In addition to what is already said about personality characteristics, there is one exceedingly important point. Although we have no accurate information concerning their onset, it seems that spells of moodiness on the part of the delinquent had been noted at home—silence, lack of response to joking, and what the sisters called "the blues" were symptoms that he presented. No periods of elation were mentioned, but much was made by the sisters of the boy's hyperactivity at times when he did not seem morose. Another matter of some interest was the strong tendency to blush easily which the boy showed when he was teased about girls or when conversing with women. The control was perfectly at ease under similar circumstances. At the correctional school from which the delinquent had escaped there had been much concern about him because of his mood swings. The psychiatrist noted periods of depression; the boy stated that he had difficulty in thinking and was desperately unhappy because he was homesick and apprehensive of death coming to himself or to some member of his family. Earlier and at this time no deep soundings could be taken of the boy's emotional experiences or causes for his attitudes and behavior. Though it was impossible to make a thoroughgoing study, cyclothymic if not definite manic-depressive tendencies were evident.

BECAUSE of the paucity of the material obtained by interviews with the boy we were only able to query: did the boy feel that he was less loved by his mother, did he have a sense of guilt because he turned to delinquency after her death and so was unworthy of her? We know that he must have realized his father's rejection of him; was any of his behavior in strong reaction to this? Did he have conflict about some experiences unknown to us?

In other terms, added to the constitutional or functional basis of his cyclothymia, were there deep emotional disturbances of any kind? It certainly seemed so, though specific knowledge of them was not forthcoming. The extent of his emotional peculiarities is shown by his pronounced fluctuations while in the institutions—there in periods of depression he maintained that he was unhappy about his home conduct and that in being shut up he was facing a situation most unpleasant for him; yet at other times in this same situation he was unduly elated. He most certainly was suffering from an affective psychosis.

H

One of twins, sixteen years old, had once been in a detention home on a minor charge of larceny and the police reported that many complaints had been entered against him but had not been pressed—we wondered whether this was because the boy had a relative who was on the police force. The lad became very confidential with us and told of having been engaged during the last five years in many delinquencies that his family knew nothing about. With companions there had been much stealing from stores by rather clever methods. The group had taken all sorts of articles and disposed of them for cash; they had discussed holding up a store keeper with a gun in order to get the contents of the cash box, but though they had a gun they never carried out this plan. They stole a good many bicycles and sold them, often after interchanging the parts. On one occasion the crowd had the idea of picking pockets. The delinquent succeeded in abstracting ten dollars from a man's pocket. A couple of older boys in this gang had been convicted and sentenced, but our lad was almost never caught. The list of his delinquencies was extensive; he believes, for example, that at least fifteen times he succeeded in getting away with valuable articles through entering the back of stores while the other members of his crowd engaged the attention of the clerks in front.

The control was a boy of thoroughly good reputation, never known to have been in delinquency of any sort.

These twins were born two years after the mother's second marriage and ten years later than any of their half-siblings—the mother had quite given up the idea that she would ever have any more children. Their father did not want any progeny and the pregnancy was unwelcome to the mother. The control was born first with normal labor and an hour or two later with a very difficult instrumental delivery the future delinquent came into the world. The latter weighed only two and a half pounds, could not nurse at the breast, but on bottle feeding thrived fairly well. The control weighed five pounds, took the breast easily, and was nursed until he was fourteen months old. During childhood the twins had pretty much the same diseases but at eleven years when they were both ill the delinquent had a complication of troubles from which he made a much poorer recovery than his brother.

Our examination showed both to be four inches short for their age-norm, with weight barely up to average for their height. The control appeared to be in quite good physical condition, but the delinquent was somewhat anaemic, had many badly carious teeth, nasal obstruction from an injury, and showed moderate facial asymmetry. In complexion they were quite different.

They were still in school, the control being in the ninth grade, doing passing work although his I.Q. was only 82. He had been a very industrious boy in school, well-regarded by his teachers. He was right-handed. The delinquent was in the sixth grade with a poor school record both for academic achievement and behavior. At times he had been very defiant toward the teachers. We found that he was left-handed, stuttered slightly, had much difficulty with language, and had an I.Q. of 76.

The delinquent was rather unusually strong for his size and good at athletics, but to most people he appeared to be unsocial, quiet, and stolid. He demanded little and showed very little response to either praise or blame. He was reticent and bashful to the extent of not being willing at home to sit at the table if there were company, even though only relatives. His brother-in-law characterized him as "bull-headed and stubborn," but we saw no signs of this nor was it confirmed by his mother. With her he was not demonstrative, but was obedient and together with his brother showed her a good deal of sympathy in her troubles. He had some little manual dexterity and his mother reported that he took much comfort in wood-working and in playing with the dog. She regarded him as being very unsocial with boys—as a matter of fact she knew very little about his companionship.

The control was not so adept at sports, but was thoroughly at ease with company and with boy friends, conversing very easily. Emotionally he was well-controlled and showed good insight. At home he was a great reader and very helpful to his mother. He was very loyal to her and to his twin, being exceptionally sympathetic with the latter.

The mother had married a second alcoholic husband; by the first she had had five children, all girls. Her second husband was a steady worker and good earner but drank heavily, spending much money on drink and had very little to do with the children. To his wife he was at time extremely abusive, so much so that occasionally the police had to be called in to quell the disturbance. The mother was a poorly educated, rather sickly woman who in her early years had been a servant. She herself was one of twins. She was a tenacious individual, with a homely philosophy, preachy to her husband, very much attached to the twins whom she still called "my little boys." Her affections had been given equally to them and she felt the necessity for fighting a good many battles on behalf of the delinquent, both at school and with the neighbors. Not having a husband that she could love she gave much of herself to the twins, perhaps somewhat overdoing the protective attitude. Possibly this may have been partly based on a sense of guilt due to the fact that when pregnant with them she had contemplated abortion; besides now that her older children were married the twins were all that she had in life. She had tried to keep them close at home and to have good recreation for them. Through her thrift the family owned a small immaculately kept cottage on the outskirts of town. The twins had often urged her to leave their father, but she endured his abuse and did everything to keep the family together.

The delinquent seemed glad to have the psychiatrist for a confidant and told a long story of delinquent and really criminal associations. He had been meeting a very bad gang of boys and young men in the evenings and with these entered into and continued in delinquency. When he was quite young, he was found too rough by his brother's friends and their mothers would come out and tell him to go home. He would retort that they were made of sugar and walk away. Then because he was active and adept he found much favor with a delinquent crowd. In very naïve fashion he said, when telling about their delinquencies and especially about his successful picking of a pocket,

"I was the slipperiest, they patted me for it and it made me feel good and I wanted to do it again." The boy made very clear that he obtained great satisfactions from the thrill of the delinquent activities—"I got going just for the fun of it; it wasn't for the money because my mother always used to give me plenty."

The school situation that the mother had made much of because she thought that the boy had been unfairly treated was sized up by him very largely in terms of affronts that he had received. He maintained that a teacher in reading had made fun of him and told the other pupils that he was a "dumb bell" —"she never did like me." He didn't know how to dance and didn't want to and he insisted that another teacher smacked his face because he said so. He was put in an ungraded school after the first three years and hated that. His whole school career after those first years had been most unfortunate—while his brother was getting along well. He developed much phantasy life about being on a ship or being a forest ranger. Then after his gang contacts he began daydreaming about being a gangster in Chicago, having a big car, and robbing stores and banks with machine guns. "I would imagine I would get away with the money and buy a yacht and an aeroplane."

There seems to have been no difference between the delinquent and the control in their feelings and attitudes toward the mother and father—they detested the latter because of his drunken habits and abuse and they both loved and sympathized with their mother. The delinquent said that he went to church with his mother and brother, but it didn't help him. He as well as his mother felt that some change had come over him through illness at eleven years from which he did not recover well. She put it that he always seemed "faggy" after that. He thought that the experience made him bashful, inclined to worry and be apprehensive.

In this case we see mainly the deep sensing of inferiorities in school experiences, with the thwartings of normal desires for recognition, such as his brother had. The type of his reactions to these discomforts stands out clearly in his story—he obtained tremendously satisfying substitutive compensations through recognition for his delinquent skills from a delinquent crowd. Besides this he plainly verbalized the pleasurable thrills of delinquent adventure. The control had no such unfortunate school experiences or feelings of inadequacy to meet and hence had not the same reasons for entering into delinquency.

CAN there be any doubt from the above contrasts in the emotional experiences and attitudes of these twins that a new outlook upon causes is imperative? It is needed for discernment of the significance of delinquency as it appears in the behavior pattern of any given individual. If knowledge of causes is essential for development of the best methods of treatment, as it is elsewhere in science, then an entirely new orientation in this field of genetics is indispensable. The more objective data concerning the delinquent's life and the various social pressures upon him are rather easily knowable and may be important factors in the production of his delinquency. But it is clear that there are more fundamental considerations and that we must shift the emphasis of our studies and pay more attention to the emotional implications of human relationships. Herein will lie the guiding principle of a new orientation.

CHAPTER VIII

COMPARISON OF EMOTIONAL EXPERIENCES DELINQUENTS AND CONTROLS

IN the process of making final analyses of the gathered data, we have been confronted with the inescapable fact that in most instances there is much more to the origins of delinquent behavior than appears when only the upper strata of causations are tapped. In well-nigh every case when the various individuals involved in the family situation —parents, other relatives, delinquents, and controls—told their own stories, gradually there was exposure of deeper and stronger roots, the tremendous importance of which for the first and continuing appearance of delinquency could not be denied.

To what extent these deeper causations were to be descried in the emotional experiences of the delinquents is partly indicated in our discussion of those who lived in family situations that apparently were favorable. Our studies of the twins brings into sharp focus the affective elements that played forceful parts in the life dramas of the delinquents as compared to the controls.

When our analyses of the data concerning family attitudes and emotional experiences were set down for all the delinquents and controls in parallel columns, the contrasts shown were amazing. Hence it comes that in weighing all possible causes for delinquency we have been tremendously impressed by the prevalence of profoundly felt emotional disturbances among the delinquents. These disturbances indubitably played a large part in the origin and growth of their delinquent tendencies. Equally convincing it was to find that studies of the controls failed in a great majority of the instances to reveal any such inner stresses. The evident vast importance of this whole matter has led us to take great pains in appraising the data contained in our records; indeed we have repeated these appraisals at intervals, three times rechecking our findings.

It finally appears that no less than *91 per cent of the delinquents* gave clear evidence of being or having been very unhappy and discontented in their life circumstances or extremely disturbed because of emotion-provoking situations or experiences. In great contradistinction we found similar evidences of inner stresses at the most in *only 13 per cent of the controls*. And here it should be said that in our concern not to overstate the contrasts we have ruled out cases in which emotional discomforts seemed comparatively mild (see appendix to this chapter and also to Chapter VI) and have included controls about whom there was some doubt concerning whether or not to any considerable degree they had suffered emotional stresses. Through assembling all of our gathered facts and evaluating them quantitatively as well as qualitatively a highly important conclusion has been reached:

Comparison of the emotional experiences and emotional reactions of delinquents and controls shows by far the greatest difference that we have been able to discover between the two groups.

Now what have we discovered to be the nature and types of these inner stresses and their causes? With all the variations in causes of unhappiness and emotional discomfort there is some difficulty in classifying them, but modern psychiatric concepts are extremely helpful for organization of data concerning emotional life. As in nearly all formulations there are some overlappings and the boundaries of distinctions are sometimes foggy, but the central ideas are essentially clear and practically useable. Then, of course, some individuals may have more than one type of emotional disturbance as in the following instance.

An unhealthy, poorly muscled boy of fifteen, after having been taken to court by his mother because of his refusal to go to school and because he had repeatedly struck her, joined in gang stealing. We discovered that he had suffered a terrific emotional upset at 13 when he revealed that his hypersexual stepfather had long been having sex relations with his sister, two years younger. Earlier this boy had been much spoiled by his mother and there had been close affectional ties between them. The painful situation thus created led the mother to take an ambivalent attitude toward the boy's step-father. whose relationships with her had been very satisfactory, and a rejective attitude toward the boy after his testimony in court had been largely responsible for the man's sentence to prison. The boy, conscious of the change in her feeling toward him and, through his knowledge of the sex affairs going on in the household, beset by unfortunate phantasies about his mother, began to display violence toward her and to be otherwise delinquent. This completely estranged her from him and he strongly felt rejected by her. Besides this he was intensely jealous of his sister who had taken the whole matter very calmly—she and the mother largely identifying themselves with each other. The boy also developed much mental conflict and guilt feeling about arousal of his own sex impulses and the adolescent phantasies accompanying them. Gradually there was added a great sense of inadequacy or inferiority because of the family scandal, his own physical weakness, and his school failure incident to his emotional and physical condition.

For the lesson it teaches we may note that though some of the sources of this boy's stresses must have been known through newspaper publicity and though his discomforts were so apparent, neither the school people when he began to show insubordination nor the truant officer seem to have had any conception that this boy's emotional life was the essential cause of his misconduct.

A few other illustrations of the great divergencies of the emotional experiences of the delinquents as compared to the controls will serve to reinforce this point. We offer them in the form in which the studies were finally worked up—by the parallel column method—it being necessary, of course, to utilize condensations and abbreviations. However the salient facts are given, as well as the psychiatric interpretations.

Nieder — January 1931

Fa. died 1919 at 27; mechanic; b. Germany; grammar sch. educ'n in U.S. Industrious, good earner, devoted husband. Mo. 38; b. U.S., Italian parentage; 1st yr. H.S.; to work early to help own family; at 16 had illeg. daughter. Since husband's death known favorably to charitable agencies—a good Mo., tries to handle chrn. intelligently, splendid housekeeper; neatly kept small apt., fair neighborhood. Family: Mo. and the 2 boys. Girl lived with mat. gdpts. till 1920, then taken by Mo. boys told she was own sister; model child; blonde; mar. 1928. Mo. much attached to John, wants his affection, wants to keep him a child, some spoiling; sacrifices herself greatly for her children; much guilt abt. illeg. child. Heredity negative.

John—b. 1916	Charles—b. 1914
Severe delq'y began 11—often stlg. from home, even rent money. Truancy; rnwy twice. Later stole consid. sum from employer, forged checks, rnwy to Phila.	*Only delq'y petty pilfering from fruit stands when small boy. Very honest and reliable.*
Sickly preg. Diffic. birth, cord around neck. Bottle fed after 2 mos. Very quiet baby. Early walking and talking. Illnesses and underwt. in early childhood.	Less sickly preg. Instru. delivery, head contusion, lanced at 1 mo. Bottle after 1 mo. Quiet baby. Severe diphth. at 2, long in hosp. Cardiac at 5, 2 yrs. in hosp.—good recovery but small and nervous.
Severe enuresis to 10, occasional to 14.	No enuresis.
Normal size and nutr. Fair strength. Mature appearance and dev. Odd looking, long face, very dark hair, very sober expression. Weak voice.	Normal ht., slight underwt. Strong. Heart, etc., normal. Rather sharp, handsome features, firm, pleasant expression. Curly light hair.
I.Q. 126. Many tests well done. Diffident.	I.Q. 100. Smiling, pleasant worker.

Normally advanced in sch. but dissatisfied with course. Mo. says he learns too quickly.	Sch. retd'n acct. illness. Thru 6th gra., then to work. Sch. rept: slow worker.
Personality: Active in sports, no close friends, wanders alone, self-consc. abt. appearance, never affectionate, sulks, resents authority, always seems repressed and unhappy. Truthful. Never confiding—Mo. and bro. say they do not know him. Reads much; avoids church; cares only for cat.	Personality: Normally active but tires easily. Complains of getting nervous and irritable. Likes a crowd. Has good chums. Assumes responsibility. Confidential, loyal. Very friendly. Reads much. Fond of church. Always seemed old for his years. Has tried to play Fa. rôle with John.
Easily gets in with bad crowd, even in sports, in clubs but no contin. interests.	No interest in sports. Early wanted to work and get more training for good job.

CONTRASTING EMOTIONAL EXPERIENCES

Feels was too dependent on Mo. Great ambivalence toward her. Has long dwelled on different appearance from siblings, his dark hair, sensed something wrong about parentage, that perhaps he is the illeg. child. Severe conflict, never expressed. Feels isolated, inferior, and in comparison to bro. has no status in family.	Was favorite of Fa., much upset by his death, said to be the image of him. Much satisfaction in Mo's reliance on him, earning capacity, and nice friends.

MacKay   October 1930

Scotch-Irish, fairly intelligent, honest parents. Hered. neg. Fa. 38, sickly, intense worker, irritable, great rages, terribly disappointed in U.S. M. 36, unhappy with husb., high temper, overcleanly, outside employment. Lost property, now tenement in poor district, 4 chrn. Wm. oldest, always much contention abt him, F. whips, M. scolds, says he is like his F., boy snarls but parents curiously ambivalent towards boy. F. fonder of other chrn who are controlled, well-mannered.

William—b. 1916	James—b. 1918
Delqy began at 7. Excess. stlg for yrs. Truancy. Slept away from home for days. Burglaries with companions. Took autos. Became leader of very notorious gang.	*Never delqt.*

Unhappy pregy. Normal birth, large baby, nursed long but cried much. Hard to manage. Rupture and opern at 3. Appendicitis at 11.

Normal pregy and birth. Smaller, nursed shorter time, quiet baby, abscess of jaw at 4, 2 mos. in hosp.

4 in. short, fair nutr.; strong; infected tonsils. Firm small features, often hard, sullen, aggressive expression.

3 in. short, good nutr.; fair strength; infected tonsils; defec. vision. Pleasant features, friendly expression, passive.

I.Q. 90. Fair sch. work, 1 yr. behind. Always hated sch. teachers.

I.Q. 105. In same grade as bro. Fond of sch.

Personality: Very active, restless, impetuous, high-strung, varies quick enthusiasms with being unhappy and non-coop. Much pleasure in leading others. Bitter, cynical abt dishonesty and "pull" everywhere, even in courts. Sometimes well mannered. Befriends unfortunate boys, generous to beggars. Writes terribly vindictive letters even to F. Hates scouts, clubs, scornful of church. Self confident, secretive, suspicious that people "gyp" him. Some pride in making things to sell. Many ideas of delqy from older boys and men, thinks of being successful criminal. Sneers at bro's good behav.

Personality: Slow moving, a few good friends, brings them to house. Always friendly and placid. Bookworm. Desires education. Likes church clubs, wants to be priest. Always reliable, model boy.

CONTRASTING EMOTIONAL EXPERIENCES

Sure for many yrs. that he is rejected and hated; in turn hates all authority. Disgust at family friction and circumstances. Wants love (nice to little sisters). Jealous of bro's standing in family. Once in burst of confidence to us told of long hating F. enough to kill him, of wanting his M's love tho she "snooped" on him; after all he cannot believe that she loves James better, tho F. does.

Satisfied with family relationships tho some contempt for F. when he occ'ly drinks. Avoids family fracas by reading and doing sch. work. Always secure in feeling loved.

Dale May 1930

Amer. family. F. d. 1917 at 40, mentally abnormal, diag. unknown. Pat. uncle psychotic. M. 43, much overweight, fairly intelli-

Comparison of Emotional Experiences

gent, jolly, extrovert, much beloved, good housekeeper, dominant, mar. again in 1920. Stepf. steady, fair earner, kindly, considerate, leaves discip. to wife. No chrn of his own. Cottage in shabby district. 4 chrn, girl fin. H.S., now clerk, good character; younger sister very large and strong. Pleasant household, all fond of each other, much merry bantering. M. earlier overprotective and very affectionate with Edw. Since trouble tried to manage him by jocular taunts, advice and oversight. Really concerned, wants him to be man but still under control. Stepf. tries to be helpful to him.

Edward—b. 1914	Frank—b. 1913
Never delqt till 14. With compans stlg. from stores, misappropn 2 autos, rnwy to N.Y., hid revolver for older "crook."	*Non-delqt.*
Pregy, birth, devel't normal. Never severely ill.	Equally normal.
Trifle short, norm. nutr. good muscles, mod. defect vision, won't wear glasses, many carious teeth, rather immature features, selfcons. expression.	Consid. taller, big and strong, healthy, heavy features, inarticulate.
Fussy eater, much coffee, poor diet, keeps late hours, restless sleep.	Normal healthy habits.
I.Q. 102 (earlier sch. I.Q. 123) 3rd yr H.S. Considered capable but last 2 yrs. fluctuating effort. Princ. tried to help, but finally expelled.	I.Q. 95, plodder in sch. Left 2nd yr H.S. to go to work.
Personality: Always sensitive. Before adol. obedient, warm hearted, obliging, demonstrative, very reliable, never crowd boy, rather effeminate. Recently more restless, only 2 or 3 compns, tough boys. Becomes discontented, sulky, grumbling, insubordinate, selfish, overly quiet at times, very obstinate. At periods talkative, boastful, "wise cracks," bluffing. Spells of religiosity. In summer likes working. Recent instability and moods suggest almost adol. psychosis.	Personality: Fairly active but slow, doesn't make friends easily, much at home, stable emotions, no change at adol. "No personality." No interest in church. Reads much unselectively. No interest in sports or girls. Steady worker. Quietly contented. Particularly thru his work feels adequate.

CONTRASTING EMOTIONAL EXPERIENCES

Earlier M. fixation, now floundering wish for emancipation conflicting with desire not to grow up. Ambivalent to M, now resents her domination. Her extrovert qualities grate on his somewhat introvert characteristics. Some inferiority about size (younger sister larger than he) and former effeminacy.	No M. fixation, never overcontrolled or overprotected by her. All along regarded as more of a man. Early became friendly with stepf., with whom he somewhat identified himself. Is afraid of getting into trouble (meeting same type of compns. as bro., breaks off with them suddenly). Quite satisfied with work and home life.

Now we may offer a statement of our total findings relative to the emotional disturbances of the 96 delinquents discovered to be suffering from them. The data, without forcing them for the purposes of this exposition, fall into well-recognized psychiatric categories through utilizing all the practical, non-theoretical concepts of human relationships and of inner mental states that are warranted by the facts. The types and the enumeration of such emotional disturbances may be presented as follows, but it must be remembered that the same individual may show more than one type of discomfort:

(a) Feeling keenly either *rejected, deprived, insecure, not understood* in affectional relationships, unloved, or that love has been withdrawn—46 cases.

(b) Deep feeling of being *thwarted* other than affectionally; either (a) in normal impulses or desires for self-expression or other self-satisfactions, (b) in unusual desires because earlier spoiled, or (c) in adolescent urges and desires —even when (as in 5 cases) desire for emancipation had been blocked only by the individual's counteractive pleasure in remaining childishly attached—28 cases.

(c) Feeling strongly either real or fancied *inadequacies or inferiorities* in the home life, in school, or in relation to companionship or to sports—46 cases.

(d) Intense feelings of *discomfort about family dishar-*

monies, parental misconduct, the conditions of family life, or parental errors in management and discipline—34 cases.

(*e*) Bitter feelings of *jealousy* toward one or more siblings, or feelings of being markedly discriminated against because another in the family circle more favored—31 cases.

(*f*) Feelings of confused unhappiness due to some deep-seated, often repressed, *internal mental conflict*—expressed in various kinds of delinquent acts which often are seemingly unreasonable—17 cases.

(*g*) Conscious or unconscious *sense of guilt* about earlier delinquencies or about behavior which technically was not delinquency; the guilt sense directly or indirectly activating delinquency through the individual's feeling of the need of punishment (in nearly every instance this overlaps with the last category)—9 cases.

SINCE emotional experiences loom so large in obvious causal relationships to delinquency, the reader surely has curiosity, first, about how we account for the delinquency in those 9 cases evidencing no strong emotional discomforts. Now we do not say that in these instances there were no discontents—that would be going too far. We merely state that such studies as we were able to make did not reveal in these cases any marked inner stresses. As may be seen in the schedule for these 9 cases at the end of the chapter, there were various factors playing a part in the drama of causation—mainly social pressures deriving from poverty, poor family standards, lack of supervision, ideas of delinquency received from companions, etc.—with very little to counterbalance on the positive or constructive side. As we review these cases we find it most interesting to note that the treatment undertaken for them and their families proved, with one exception, to be highly successful.

Second, were no emotional disturbances detected in the series of controls? It goes without saying that practically every child has had unhappinesses about something—feelings of inferiority or having been deprived or thwarted in some desires—but the point is that many children, as shown by our studies of the controls, have not suffered from serious, persisting emotional maladjustments. We did find 14 controls who evidently had experienced some considerable degree of emotional discomfort, but in every instance they were able to find counterbalancing satisfactions. Either they found some other affectional relationship which substituted for the one barred to them, or their feeling of inadequacy in some direction was compensated for by satisfactory achievement in other ways, or distress about a family situation was made more tolerable for them by active allegiance to one of the parents. It might be thought that the delinquents also had opportunities for achieving satisfactions to offset emotional stress, but the ascertainable fact was that either circumstances totally prevented compensatory adjustments or that the established reactive tendencies of the delinquent individual or of others in the family circle did not permit satisfying emotional responses.

FACTORS IN 9 CASES OF DELINQUENTS WITHOUT MARKED EMOTIONAL STRESS

Boy with no conscience about stealing at which parents connived; great poverty; older half brother stole with him.

Boy idle, wanted adventure, misappropriated cars for "joy riding."

Boy from poor but very good family living in area of high delinquency; extremely susceptible to suggestions of notorious delinquents.

Boy much in street life; father dead, mother working; absorbed criminal ideas from companions.

Boy with perfectly good record previously becomes very lonely through the loss of a friend; makes a new acquaintance who proves to be a delinquent of long standing; engages with him for a few weeks in orgy of wild adventure by breaking into houses.

Boy from family of very poor standards, placed in institution, learned sex perversions, engages in them with more aggressive companion.

Boy, active, gregarious, very insufficient outlets, economic stress; much influenced by delinquent companions.

Girl, very easy going, much like easy-going mother; family poor, feeling sorry for underprivileged orphaned companion repeatedly aided her in shoplifting.

Girl, daughter of a moralizing shop-lifting mother, probably partially identifies herself with the mother as under the influence of an older girl engages on several occasions with this companion in shoplifting.

CHAPTER IX

THE MEANINGFULNESS OF DELINQUENCY FOR THE INDIVIDUAL—A NEW ORIENTATION

THE discovery that the emotional experiences and attitudes of our delinquents differ significantly from those of the controls and with much greater frequency than any other ascertained contrast brings us to a further step in the interpretation of delinquent behavior. Since delinquency appears clearly to be a reaction to emotional disturbances and discomforts, the delinquency itself must in some fashion be especially meaningful for the individual of whose behavior it is a part. The interpretations of this meaningfulness constitute the second of the new orientations foreshadowed in Chapter II.

The enumeration of the disturbances of the feeling life characterizing the delinquents and the given examples place squarely before us the material for an entirely new outlook on the activating forces of delinquent behavior. The frustrations of the fundamental urges, desires, and wishes which belong to the normal stream of life's activities are plainly to be seen. More explicitly, the desires for human relationships which are satisfying as they afford affectional acceptance and security, recognition of the individual as a personality, realization of social adequacy, opportunity for satisfactory accomplishment, for independence, new experiences, and for outlets and possessions have somehow been thwarted. The individual has found himself blocked in any one or more of these urges or wishes.

The obstructions have engendered feelings of dissatisfaction, deprivation, inadequacy, jealousy, or inner conflict which themselves are the discomforts antedating the delinquent behavior. But our reorientations must concern themselves not only with the dynamics antecedent to the delinquency, but also with the essential meaning of the act itself. Though obstructions to fundamental wishes can readily be interpreted as affectional thwartings, ego deprivations, or threats to ego-satisfactions, the question still remains—why is the reaction that of delinquent behavior? It might be and often is manifested in other ways. As a general phenomenon delinquency is evidently consequent upon frustrations, yes, but for the individual himself delinquency must have some basic though often unverbalized specific meaning. To put the question in another way: what subjective value, conscious or unconscious, has the delinquent behavior for the delinquent himself? This subjective value may be something quite different from the estimates made as behavior is viewed objectively by others.

In answering, we believe that the immediate significance of delinquency for the individual is susceptible of interpretation—and without the danger of introducing large elements of error because in nearly all of our case histories the nature of the delinquent reactions is writ large. Indeed occasionally the delinquent himself expressed to us his insight into the special meaning for him of delinquency as a reaction.

Without making our classifications parallel the categories of emotional disturbances given in the previous chapter, we can describe the types of reactions represented by delinquency as follows:

(*a*) Attempt to avoid, even as a temporary measure, the unpleasant situation by *escape* or *flight* from it.

(*b*) Attempt to achieve substitutive *compensatory satisfactions* through delinquent activities. These satisfactions include the thrill of delinquent adventure and the gratification at obtaining special recognition or attention, perhaps even notoriety, as a delinquent. In some instances material gains figure as compensation for deprivation.

(c) Attempt to strengthen or *bolster up the ego* wounded by feelings of inadequacy or inferiority. The aim then is to obtain *recognition and status* with the delinquent crowd; or, if the offender is more solitary in tendencies, by the individual proving to himself that he really is courageous and can in some way play a spirited rôle. This "masculine protest" we found to be a not uncommon reaction with some previously effeminate or feminized boys. Said one such lad, "They thought I was no good so I went out to show a cockeyed world that I was a regular guy."

(d) Attempt to get certain ego-satisfactions through direct and conscious or even unconscious expression of *revenge attitudes*—perhaps through hidden desire to punish parents or others by conduct that will make life difficult for them.

(e) Attempt to gain a *maximum of self-satisfaction*, to inflate the ego, by generally aggressive, antisocial attitudes, that is, by the exhibition of definite hostilities and antagonisms to authority.

(f) *Response to instinctual urges* felt to be thwarted. While this response may be exhibited in sexual misbehavior, more notably in our delinquents we have discovered the attempt to satisfy the urge for independence and emancipation which normally flares up as an adolescent phenomenon.

(g) The wish for punishment was clearly discernible in a few instances and suspected in others. This *seeking punishment*—delinquent behavior possibly offering an opportunity for being punished—was always a response to a conscious or unconscious sense of guilt.

BUT even now with our new appreciation of the meaningfulness of delinquency as a reaction to frustrations, there still remains a question of considerable interest and importance: just why is delinquency selected as a mode of reactive behavior? Our studies make it readily apparent that delinquency affords a vehicle for expression of reactions to emotional discomforts, but, as we said before, there are many other ways of expressing dissatisfactions; delinquency is one mode.

In almost no instances does delinquency follow upon a simple and conscious mental process—ordinarily the individual does not say to himself, "Through delinquency I will have my revenge," or "By being delinquent I will seize what immediate gratifications I can to make up for deprivations." Usually the act is engaged in by the delinquent without verbalizing to himself, indeed without conscious awareness that he is engaging in an evasive, substitutive, or compensatory form of behavior. It is rather that delinquency offers itself as a vehicle for reactive urges because ideas of delinquency have already been a part of the thought content of the individual.

It is apparent that ideas about delinquency are common property of old and young; through many sorts of communication knowledge of it is everywhere prevalent. Delinquency is such a common denominator of behavior in some neighborhoods that even very young children are acquainted with many of its forms—the invitation to delinquency is readily gained from many sources.

The point is that while we discover emotional disturbances to be such a great incentive to delinquent behavior, yet the part that the ideational life plays cannot be neglected. At the same time this part should not be overemphasized, as it is by those who place the entire blame for the prevalence of juvenile delinquency upon crime movies or the reading of detective stories. If even a small percentage of those who saw stories of crime in the movies or of those who read "pulp magazine" accounts of criminals were delinquents, the statistics for juvenile delinquency would be a hundred fold what they are. Yet ideas derived from the environment do fashion the form that youthful activities take in delinquency as in sports. Marked illustrations of this are to be found.

For example, school truancy which is such a common phenomenon in this country occurs hardly at all in Switzerland because it does not fit in with the ideas of the children there. In Finland fighting with knives, which is never seen here, belongs to the traditional ideas of the people to the extent that a considerable proportion of the boys in a correctional school are sent there, we have been informed, because of homicides resulting from such fighting. And can anyone doubt that many of our particular national forms of delinquency and crime, such as "hold-ups," result from the common acquaintance with ideas held about such offenses, discernible even in the everyday play of small boys?

With all the ideas of delinquency that in our modern world pour in upon the young individual from many sources the acceptance of these ideas as offering a mode of behavior which may be pursued is, as we have shown, dependent upon whether or not there are other sufficient satisfactions. Under the stress of emotional discomforts, even the discomforts of "nothing else to do," the invitation to dwell upon and to accept such ideas is especially great. Then certainly there is more ready acceptance of ideas of delinquency if they accord with what might be termed special needs of the individual, as in the cases of those hyperactive, overrestless boys described earlier, who in their emotional life had found frustrations. Under certain circumstances it may be healthier and more normal to join in with the activities and imbibe the ideas of a delinquent crowd than to be a withdrawing, soft, effeminate "mother's boy" or, as in instances already mentioned, to mope at home and develop an abnormal phantasy life.

AGAIN from our parallel column method of condensing case records illustrations may be offered. Here, in addition to the contrasting emotional experiences emphasized in the last chapter, we present interpretations of the delinquent behavior in terms of its meaningfulness for the individual himself. These are concrete examples of the utilization of our new orientation concerning the specific dynamics of delinquency.

Laner — July 1930

F. 50, mechanic, good earner. M. 50, motherly, very good manager and housekeeper. Parents mixed ancestry, came from eastern Can. province. Both healthy, strong characters, high standards, religious, happy marriage, forging ahead, thrifty, intent on chrn having best possible educ'n. Own home. All boys in magazine distributing business under charge of eldest who organized it. Extraordinarily fine ambitious family with much good feeling between them. 4 chrn; 2 eldest boys preparing for college, one younger than Geo. regarded as very promising and somewhat favored on that account. All chrn big, strong, good looking.

George—b. 1915	Donald—b. 1914
1 yr ago stole fancy skates. More recently forged and collected on check found in office when delivering magazines, also later opened envelopes in another office and took money. Bought play things mostly.	*Always honest, tho knew about skates and kept silent.*
Normal dev. history. Long nursing. Always seemed healthy, but fatigues more easily than bros. Overweight for 3 or 4 yrs. Craving for sweets.	Norm. dev. history. Long nursing. Always healthy. Careful eater.
Norm. ht. 50 lbs overwt, high-pitched voice, retarded sex dev. etc. (Bros all early puberty) Diag. by thoro endocrine study, hypopituitary. Defective vision, no glasses.	Big, strong, stout within normal limits. Good features. Wears glasses.
I.Q. 108 (later 116). Very rapid alert worker. Pleasantly responsive.	I.Q. 99. Very serious worker. Especially good in mech'l tests.
1st yr H.S., poor marks, well liked.	2nd yr H.S., taking technical course, doing very well.
Personality: Active but tires easily, impulsive, changeable, pleasure loving, talkative, care-free, frank, different from bros in these respects, even-tempered. Worked in bro's business since 9, little time for companionship.	Personality: Active, steady, quiet, planful, studies hard, reserved, inarticulate, ambitious. Worked in bro's business since 10, little time for companionship.

Interpretations: For 2 or 3 yrs mainly on acct endocrine disorder Geo. has felt inadequate to meet high ambitions of family who have tried to spur him on. Has felt different and isolated in fam. circle.—Attempt to get substitutive satisfactions thru stlg money for young boyish possessions which according to family standards were silly and useless. . . . Felt thwarted in normal desires and impulses, fond of sports but no time to indulge. Worked outside sch. for yrs, didn't have such privileges as other boys. Christmas coming, wouldn't have much.—Revengeful display of impulsive aggressiveness; he would get things anyhow. . . . Strongly felt discriminated against; younger bro., "a popular hero," favored. Discouraged abt it.—Hostile attitude for a time; knocked his bro. about. Then ephemeral floundering aggressive impulses to get compensatory satisfactions thru having his own pleasures.

Stanowsky October 1931

Parents Polish. F. 44, little educ., quiet, hard worker, seldom drunk, apparently stable on low level. At times worries abt chrn, feels helpless abt them. M. 36, no educn, proby subnormal, concerned abt chrn except Helen, uses threats and strap liberally. Cottage; above poverty level; district not crowded, but many delqts. 6 chrn, 2 older boys very delqt, now in instns. Alice, 4, beautiful child much petted. No friction betw. parents; in general they care for chrn but non-understanding, no ambitions for them, some advantages in home, some books, etc. M. bemoans fate of older bros. F. and M. rely on Maria, praise her much. Alice is "queen" of household. M. curiously indifferent to Helen, when away does not even look for her, beats her black and blue, rarely mentions her.

Helen—b. 1918	Maria—b. 1915
Twice in court. Stlg money, etc., from neighbors, earlier a bicycle. Much truancy. Stolen from stores, from people on st., articles from home. Away over night sev'l times, once away for a week, slept in doghouse.	*Non-delqt.*
Pregy and birth easy. Nursed abt. 1 yr. Always fairly healthy. Occasional enuresis. Very short but norm nutrn, defec. vision, wears glasses. Good health. Pretty child, appears young for yrs.	Develop. history equally negative. Nursed equally long. No enuresis.
I.Q. 92. Excellent attention and perseverance. Left-handed, very good eye-hand coördination.	I.Q. 93, quick worker, persevering. Right-handed.

In 6th gr. Demotions for truancy. Much dislike of certain teachers.

Personality: Active in sports, always wants to boss. Often restless. Gregarious. Irritable, quick tempered, careless abt clothes. Mischievous. Takes no household responsibilities. Readily makes friends with poor compns. Fond of little animals, mice, etc. Aggressive fighter. Hides in coal cellar, etc. Responsive and attempts to make up to other adults but unhappy with own parents. Says M's beatings make her mad, also Maria's overgoodness. Hates them and her F. when drunk, hates baby sister.

Finished 8th gr. at 15, good record in sch.

Personality: Less energetic. Does not make friends so easily. Good tempered. Hard working, does household tasks willingly, always wanted to be boy. Calm, neat, wants to be nurse, enjoys helping people. "Always good." Happy. Particular abt her friends. Speaks of being well treated and content with family.

Interpretations: Helen with every reason feels, in great contrast to Maria, thoroughly rejected, unloved—Attempts to bolster up ego by hostile, aggressive, antisocial behavior. . . . Deep feeling of inferiority at home and in sch.—Attempts compensatory satisfactions thru stlg and thru obt'g recognition with delqt compns. Also wins special attention of poor type neighbors thru staying in their house. . . . Intense feeling abt unfairness of punishments.—Flights from home. . . . Feels discriminated against and jealous of both sisters—Revenge by creating troubles for family.

Onlac November 1929

Parents Lithuanian, to U.S. just after married. F. 50, worked many yrs same place, quiet, very good standards, passive except in crises when whips Peter. M. 45, energetic, matriarch, excitable, voluble, complaining, inconsistent, great drive to control. Long owned home; with econ. stress have to rent part of it, crowded quarters. Neighborhood become congested, many delqts. 7 chrn, 2 older boys mar. live nearby; 2 sisters older, one younger than our 2 boys. Close-knit, cordial, fun-loving fam. group. Consider themselves more respectable than neighbors. Older chrn had to work early, none delqt. All centered hopes on Peter going to Yale; all spoiled him, e.g. allowed 6 clean shirts a week. The "black sheep." Still can wheedle M. but actual fights with her. Later fam. transferred college ambitions to Alexis. M. says hated Peter bec. of pain caused her at birth but always did more for him than others; overprotected inconsistently, punished bec. left-handed. At times boy beaten by F. and older bro. M. interferes.

Peter—b. 1914

Truancy and stlg at 8 yrs, formed delq'y club. Court first at 9; 6 times to date. Last 3 yrs much stlg with compns, some from home, petty burglaries, much truancy, serious stlg from employers sev'l times. Rnwy to N.Y. etc. 3 times. Great fabricator.

Painful pregy, exceedingly long and painful labor, fussy young baby, nursed 10 mos. difficult weaning, frail young child, rec'd much care. Only sev. illness pneum. at 8.

Norm. ht., wiry build, strong and healthy, carious teeth, rather delicate sharp features, often merry expression. Left-handed.

I.Q. 87, indifferent worker, very good apperceptions, some good learning powers. Left sch. at 15, 8th gr. Repeated 3rd and 4th grades. Reported lazy and mischievous. Disliked sch.

Personality: Varies greatly in energy output, sometimes very active. Gregarious but shifts friends. Varies in emotions, but no definite imbalance. Merry, vivacious, well liked acct. humorous response. Suggestible to outsiders. Likes rough compns. Movies plus. Desire for new experiences, but afraid to leave home. Vague ambitions.

Alexis—b. 1916

Never delq't; good conduct.

Norm. pregy, easy birth, quiet baby, nursed 14 mos, never severely ill.

Norm. ht, asthenic build, signs of old rickets, healthy, carious teeth, bites nails, good looking, complacent expression. Right-handed.

I.Q. 97, good apperceptions, slow, careful worker, poor in lang. and arith. 8th gr., hard worker, "good pupil" but marks not good. Very fond of sch.

Personality: More inactive. Few friends, one chum for 10 yrs. Very even tempered, docile, rather stolid, obedient, conformist, persevering, rather read and study than movies. Saving. No desire for new experience or emancipation. "Mother is always right." Definite ambitions. Regarded as the model. Delights in fam. praise.

Interpretations: Felt inadequate in sch. life when rept'd 3rd gr.—Sought substitute satisfns in delq't thrills. . . . After yrs of spoiling cd not get own way, felt deprived—Says some delq'y was in revenge for this. . . . Wants emancipation, but blocked by own fixations and dependency on M.— Tries adventure and toughness in attempt to strengthen ego. . . . Later discomfort in sch. failure—Escape in truancy. . . . Feels thwarted in ego desires to retain family position—Fabrication of exploits attention-getting device to inflate the ego. . . . Growing sense of infer'y in fam.; jealousy of Alexis.—Attempts to bolster up ego thru gaining status with delq'ts. . . . (Later when broke off with compns and sometimes doing well in work and praised by family at once stole again without need. His bro. says Peter can't stand success.—Perhaps seeking self-punishment thru unconsc. sense of guilt.) Boy insists much influenced by gangster pictures which fed ideas early gained from one compn.

CHAPTER X

THE TREATMENT PROGRAM

WHATEVER is done for delinquents or for their families that is aimed at checking delinquency may be termed treatment—there seems to be no better word. Treatment was incorporated as one of the prime objectives of this research for two main reasons: First, because it has been so amply proven that attempts to curb delinquent careers by juvenile court procedure is, in general, extremely disappointing in results. To say nothing of the frequent inefficacy of warnings and advice calculated to make the delinquent feel responsible for his own conduct, it is found that, when he has been rendered as much presumably constructive service as probation officers can give, the outcomes of such efforts to a most unfortunate extent prove to be failures.

Second, because the offender is commonly regarded as the sole unit to be worked with, we proposed to learn what could be accomplished by considering the family as the unit. Scientific attempts at modification of the behavior of biological units in other fields proceed from the standpoint that tendencies cannot be altered without taking into account environmental influences and the prior conditionings of experiences. Now the most immediate, most influential, and most conditioning environment of young human beings is that of family life and its relationships. Thus is it sensible, we asked, to expect that behavior tendencies can be reconstructed without modifying the family interrelationships that must be actively playing a part in creating the experiences and attitudes which left the young individual susceptible to the growth of delinquent ideation and behavior?

With all this in mind it seemed clear that the next steps forward in the prevention of delinquency should be work with the delinquent himself carefully aimed at meeting the causes of his troubles, while at the same time attempting therapeutic modification of the factors in family life which had been directly or indirectly producing the delinquent's tendencies.

Our project thus called for side-by-side research in causation and methods of treatment. What we were to learn about the individual and the influences of his environmental situation, especially as they involved earlier and present experiences in family life, was to be utilized as far as possible in an endeavor to bring about any desirable changes in him or in his family.

As intimated in the introductory chapter time limits later imposed upon our research prevented carrying out our original program. It was planned to proceed for three years or so with methods of treatment apparently best calculated to meet the needs of each case and each family. We proposed then to allow a considerable interval when careful stock might be taken of accomplishments, failures, and ascertained possibilities in order to reconsider techniques, reshape generalizations, and frame new orientations for another experimental period of treatment. The second period of therapy not having been possible, the present report of treatment concerns itself with the first three-year trial of procedures.

We cannot here dwell on the technical aspects of our treatment with the delinquents themselves though such efforts formed a considerable share of the work in our three centers. The nature of these efforts was dictated by the findings of thoroughgoing clinical studies in each given case and, since we had highly trained staffs who were engaged in an intensive therapeutic research with comparatively few cases, the quality of the treatment undertaken was distinctly high. The quantity and the range of therapeutic endeavor was far

The Treatment Program

beyond what any probation officer with his ordinary case load could be expected to initiate. Medical and dental needs were well taken care of; the interest of school people was enlisted whenever necessary and many beneficial school readjustments were made; recreational plans were set afoot and carried out in accord with the interests of the individual and the resources of the community; country vacations were arranged; jobs were occasionally secured; placing in foster homes for some was made possible. All these things were accomplished through the more-than-willing coöperation of professional and social organizations, including the juvenile court officials in each of the three cities.

From the figures given in the appendix of this chapter it will be seen that a rich program of effort was carried through. However, the extent of these efforts is not at all shown by the statement of numbers or percentages in which certain treatment measures were tried—for example, some delinquents required many hours of attention to the problems of their school adjustment, a few were given months of tutoring, many trips and excursions were made in order to develop hobbies and new interests, through numerous home visits and clinic contacts the aim was to develop a spirit of friendly coöperation in the delinquent himself.

In accord with their own theories, it may be that some critics will feel that greater emphasis should have been placed upon moral education, on group recreational projects, etc., or more exclusively on an intensive psychotherapeutic relationship between the delinquent and the psychiatrist; since this was, however, a first experiment in clinical responsibility for the entire treatment of a series of court cases it was deemed best not to emphasize endeavors in any one field, but rather to use any and all methods of treatment that the obvious needs of the delinquent appeared to suggest.

When the study of the case revealed emotional difficulties, as it did in so many instances, the possible values of continuing psychiatric treatment for the delinquent were always considered and attempts were made to put them into effect. The aim was to develop the delinquent's insight into the real sources of his unsocial behavior—through this and accompanying release of emotional tensions to set in action reconstruction of his emotional attitudes and his behavior tendencies. Because such treatment was rejected by the delinquent or by the parents, or because other than emotional factors appeared to be the main causes for the delinquency, or when the delinquent was quickly sent to an institution, such psycho-therapy was not attempted in 28 cases. The actual psychiatric work that was carried on may be classified as moderate in amount for 70 cases and intensive in 45. Nearly a third of the cases had ten or more psychiatric interviews and with some who were found to be suffering from deep-lying mental conflicts or who had chronically exhibited difficult conduct trends the psychiatrist spent much time, indeed, fifteen of the cases had from 25 to 75 interviews.

While the ultimate response of the offenders to these various forms of treatment is perhaps to be best judged by our report on outcomes, the immediate response in nearly all cases was thoroughly favorable. In only one case was there refusal to coöperate at all in treatment plans, and the rejection of our services in this case was due to the boy's extreme defensive attitude about the miserable conditions of his family life. The large majority undoubtedly thoroughly enjoyed contacts with psychiatrists and social workers—in fact since the disbandment of the clinics there have been many evidences of persisting friendliness. When there was not good coöperation, it was usually due to parental attitudes, although in only one case did a parent, a very abnormal individual leading a shady life, refuse to allow his children to come to the clinic. Of course it was obvious that our work to a very considerable extent had to depend upon the parents' backing, and this was not always completely forthcoming.

To persuade the delinquent to continue with psychiatric interviews was not always easy; some very evidently did not want to face facts that might reveal how deeply they felt their thwartings and deprivations—giving way to their reactive urges and impulses seemed self-expression enough for them. But, as might be expected, differences of all sorts were exhibited in attitudes and responses; for example, some of the most "hard boiled" severe offenders were willing and almost anxious to talk out their life situations and feelings.

In total a great deal of time and energy was given to the treatment of the delinquents themselves. In Detroit especially, with a larger staff and funds available for direct expenditure on the cases, an enormous amount of work other than psychiatric treatment was done. To mention only a few items in the recreational and educational program that seemed to offer therapeutic values, it may be stated that delinquents were taken on excursions to places of interest; when they were in want they were provided with clothes to make themselves presentable; special tutoring for school advancement was sometimes provided; little parties were given at the clinic; for some piano or tap dancing lessons were obtained. In Detroit foster home placing was much utilized. The New Haven clinic was much more restricted in its efforts because that city had fewer social agency resources for country vacations and for placing in foster homes than either of the other cities. However the one boys' club and the few other recreational centers were much used. Good school cooperation and understanding, so important in many instances, was much more available in Detroit and New Haven than in Boston. Each of these first two school systems was keenly alive to the problems that children present and maintained good child-study departments of their own.

COMING now to the statement of the forms of treatment that were undertaken with families, we may begin by giving some of the questions that we put to ourselves at an early stage of the development of our research: (a) Granted that family attitudes, behavior tendencies, and situations are largely involved in the production of delinquency among the children, will intensive work with families avail in checking delinquent trends? (b) Can therapeutic relationships be established through which families may be reëducated to a better understanding of their part and thereby be willing to assume responsibility for altering whatever has been at fault? (c) Or shall we find that parents or parental substitutes are too set in their ways or are too embedded in their particular social or economic *milieu* to be able to change their attitudes and behavior tendencies? Or conversely, can we find evidences that parents are alterable in essential characteristics? (d) Shall we be able to say that, if the personnel of courts included well-trained professional workers who would make deeper studies of the issues in family life, there would be enough frequency of coöperation on the part of families to lead to some considerable amount of checking of delinquency? (e) Could courts accomplish a great deal more if they were able under the law to insist on the family taking responsibility for the betterment of children's behavior? (f) Or, finally, shall we be forced to the conclusion that with existing social, economic, industrial and recreational conditions, or with group ideas or national ideologies being what they are, families cannot be expected effectively to alter situations that are fundamental in forming antisocial conduct tendencies?

Our findings that in case after case the family life and parental attitudes played such an important part in originating the behavior tendencies of the delinquent was paralleled by the discovery that the juvenile court staff in almost all instances had not been cognizant of these deeper factors, or if occasionally they had been aware of them, had not initiated treatment directed toward betterment of the essential matters. Our attack upon the problem of delinquency from the family standpoint was thus a new experience for the family.

There is an immense difference between family treatment in juvenile court cases and in the modern child guidance clinic where even with a delinquent child parents come for assistance thinking already of their own methods of upbringing as part of the problem to be solved. The resistances so common among juvenile court families are sometimes due to general ignorance or to a hopeless feeling of inability to cope with the inimical features of their economic and personal situations, but it often means that the parents have been totally unaware of and are unwilling to face the rôle which they themselves have played in forming the behavior tendencies of the delinquent. Then there are instances in which parents are not conducting their own lives properly and for this or other reasons do not wish to be disturbed. The extent to which these and other blockings confronted our efforts to deal with families in a treatment relationship is indicated in our appended list of types of reasons why treatment was found impossible with a certain proportion of the families.

Since modern ideas of parental education had almost never reached the families we dealt with, our first step had to be taken in selling ourselves as an agency that might help the family, if they were coöperative, in possibly checking further delinquency of the child. We were usually first met by the parental conception that the delinquent alone should be dealt with, or at least the delinquent and conditions outside the family life. There was almost no exception to this. The delinquent alone was at fault, or his companionship was to blame and should be broken up, or the neighborhood situation was bad and somebody should alter it. Then if in the investigative interviews it was revealed that there were unfortunate conditions in the family life that might at least be partly responsible for the delinquent's behavior, parents very frequently could not see how these things could be blamed or changed. To meet these preconceptions and the many prejudices, it was necessary for our social workers and psychiatrists to assume very tactful attitudes in a reëducative endeavor. After all when one surveys what was found in the background of these family lives, one is surprised that there was not more resistance shown to our advances.

Knowing well that in much probation and other social work the father is found difficult to influence and sometimes even to contact and yet often is the crux of some unfortunate situation in family life, we made a special effort to enlist the fathers' coöperation. Nor did we confine our therapeutic efforts to the parents if other members of the family seemed to have relationship to the delinquent's feelings and activities.

About the frame of mind in which the family was left by its experiences in the juvenile court we can do little more than generalize, though we had much concern over it in some cases. The common-sense ideal when we were to work with the family was, of course, for parents to have had it made plain to them that possibly some better understandings of the delinquent and of themselves might accomplish much— and certainly this is just as great a need if a probation officer is to deal successfully with a family. But when parents felt themselves brow-beaten, unfairly blamed, or realized that they were threatened, their attitudes toward authority were deeply impaired—and this occurred in several instances. However, conversely we were convinced that, if after a good investigation which showed parents to be at fault the court had shown a stronger hand with them, much more could have been accomplished by the court and by ourselves. These two types of weaknesses of the juvenile court in dealing with causes of delinquency as they exist in family life is well recognized by all careful students of youthful offenders.

The Treatment Program

THE treatment that in the interest of the delinquent we felt was necessary to carry out for parents and sometimes for other members of the family can be subsumed under five heads—medical, economic, educational, social, psychiatric. Feeling certain that physical ailments often lead to the display of harmful attitudes and that economic stresses create dissatisfactions and anxieties which are reflected in behavior within the family circle, we steered about 24 per cent of the parents in obtaining some form of medical care and about the same number were aided in securing financial assistance. There was some difference in these needs as they appeared for the families in the three cities. In Boston the families averaged a little better in social and economic status and many of those in poorer circumstances already had their needs taken care of by public and private hospitals and welfare agencies, so that it was necessary in only 12 per cent to undertake measures for medical and economic relief, as against 25 per cent and 33 per cent respectively for New Haven and Detroit.

The educational treatment undertaken by our social workers was mainly aimed at better care of the children, and took many directions—instructions in household budgeting; teaching better ways of managing children as, for example, when old world standards conflicted with the ideas of the young people in the family; persuading the more intelligent parents to read books on child care or even child psychology, or leading them to become acquainted with local club and other benefits for their children; inducing parents to move from a poor neighborhood or to allow the child to be placed in a foster home.

What might be termed the social treatment is more difficult to describe; it hinged greatly on establishing friendships with parents through which they received recognition and the satisfaction of feeling that someone was interested in them. Such opportunities were seized on and greatly appreciated in the vast majority of the cases.

By psychiatric treatment we mean the process by which the psychiatrist or the psychiatric social worker attempted to develop in parents or substitute parents insights into the real issues of human relationships. Another way of expressing it is to state that the goal of psychiatric treatment with parents is to develop understanding of the emotional elements involved in the display of prejudices, hates, spoilings, overprotections, shieldings, rejections, overpunishments, and all the other exhibitions of undesirable behavior toward the child. This involves some degree of close sympathetic relationship between social worker and parent.

The treatment, at least the kinds of treatment, attempted with families is indicated by the tables at the end of this chapter. To reckon up the number of hours or the number of interviews devoted to any or to all the forms of treatment would be a huge and unnecessary task. It is perhaps sufficient to say that not only scores but hundreds of hours of service have been given to not a few families in our endeavor to do as good a job as possible. Not only the social worker but frequently also the psychiatrist advised with parents; he occasionally made home visits as well as saw in his office the parent as a patient. Matters such as the parents' alcoholism or illicit sex relationships, as well as their unhappinesses, discomforts, or feelings of guilt were in many instances freely discussed. Much effort was made to win them over to realization of their own needs and urges that they might see and act upon the possibilities of remedying their own attitudes which had been unfavorably affecting the delinquents' conduct trends.

The response of parents or guardians to the kinds or levels of treatment attempted is likewise given in the appended tables. Almost none entirely rejected all types of services, but since we found so frequently that the emotional discomforts nourishing the roots of delinquent behavior involved family relationships, our attention was largely centered on reëducational and more specifically on psychiatric treatment. The unfortunate amount of rejection of this latter form of therapy and the too-frequently discovered fact that parents did not possess capacity for being helped on this level is shown in the tables.

Difficult though it was sometimes to measure, careful evaluation of parental modification at the end of the clinical service was first made by the social worker or by the psychiatrist who was mainly in contact with the case—the attitudes of both parents or of the parent who really was the one mainly involved in the establishment of the delinquent's behavior being taken as the criterion of results. Second, reevaluations have been conducted through checkings and recheckings of the recorded material and the addition of facts that have come to hand later—this secondary evaluation having been undertaken by the directors of the research who have personally known very many of the cases and who have had at hand all records. Altogether much conscientious effort has been given to making a fair estimation of the results of intensive treatment centering on family relationships and situations.

In 123 cases reconstruction of the parental attitude was clearly necessary for the solution of the delinquent's problems.[1] Of these, where treatment on various levels was attempted, the parent in 58 cases apparently was not changed for the better, even though the first response may have been favorable. That there were various reasons for our inability to modify the parent is obvious. The proportion of failure or success in the three cities has little significance. For example the Detroit clinic through having the largest staff and most funds and excellent coöperative agencies at its disposal was

1. For details concerning treatment undertaken for families and results therefrom see appendix to chapter.

able to do the most intensive work with families, but it so happens that it had to cope with the greatest amount of abnormality in parents. Then in the New Haven series there was the largest proportion of ignorant immigrant families.

Parents were modified in 65 cases, or 53 per cent of those whose attitudes were involved—not too bad a proportion considering the human material with which we had to deal. We have grouped these according to estimates of whether parents were somewhat favorably modified in essential attitudes and behavior (28 cases—23 per cent) or were definitely much modified in these respects (37 cases—30 per cent).

Next we may ask: in the 67 cases where a definite psychiatric approach was accepted by parents, what were the results in terms of modification of the parent? Again we see reason for subdividing the group. In 41 instances where the psychiatric treatment was carried on more surface or educational levels, the parent showed modification in all but four cases. These very favorable results cannot fairly be compared with the other sub-group for reasons which follow.

In the remaining 26 families a much more thoroughgoing attempt at psychiatric treatment was carried out because very deep-lying and difficult emotional situations were involved. This smaller group includes parents of some of the most serious offenders. Parents were much or somewhat modified in all but six instances.

Naturally, any ultimate evaluation of the results of treatment undertaken with families must be in terms of the extent to which delinquency of the children was checked, since this forms the central problem of our research. The correlation of outcomes with parental modifications is dealt with in the next three chapters. Here it is to be remembered that the delinquent himself has for years built up reactive tendencies, habit formation, and ways of looking at himself and the world, and that aside from the family circle he has established connections and associations which are not easy to break. Thus with regard to outcomes two treatment variables are involved—response of the delinquent to treatment, and response of the parents whenever their attitudes and behavior are implicated.

So far as the response and modification of parents and families is concerned, the net result must be considered far from discouraging if we take into account the ignorance and intellectual limitations of a considerable share of the parents as well as the specific environmental situations which enmesh them. Not a few of these parents were too thoroughly established in the patterns of their own bad living to be willing to change them, even when their behavior interfered with the essential welfare of the children. Some were too involved in marital difficulties or were dulled to other considerations by their own struggles for existence.

As a final word about our treatment program it should be added that though what was carried out represented research and consequently was largely on an experimental basis; yet as in all clinical work the desire to help the delinquents and their families was paramount. Hence, as we disbanded our clinics, we transfered the considerable number in need of further assistance to social agencies who would give continuing service.

TREATMENT OF THE DELINQUENTS

		Approximate figures
Medical and dental treatment obtained	Boston	50 per cent
	New Haven	27 per cent
	Detroit	50 per cent
Interpretation to school people with school adjustments often made and tutoring sometimes given in the clinic	Boston	52 per cent
	New Haven	60 per cent
	Detroit	94 per cent

		Approximate figures
Club or group affiliation made	Boston	60 per cent
	New Haven	50 per cent
	Detroit	80 per cent
Hobbies and interests developed	Boston	60 per cent
	New Haven	33 per cent
	Detroit	66 per cent
Aid in obtaining employment	Boston	16 per cent
	New Haven	10 per cent
	Detroit	8 per cent
Placed in foster home	Boston	23 per cent
	New Haven	6 per cent
	Detroit	42 per cent
Committed to institution during treatment period	Boston	17 per cent
	New Haven	30 per cent
	Detroit	12 per cent

No treatment done with delinquent because
    Very early sent to institution — 3 cases
    Blocked by parent or delinquent — 2 cases

Psychiatric treatment		
Not undertaken beyond first interviews (28 cases)	Boston	15 per cent
	New Haven	25 per cent
	Detroit	20 per cent
Moderate in amount (70 cases)	Boston	48 per cent
	New Haven	44 per cent
	Detroit	55 per cent
Intensive (45 cases—15 of these had from 25 to 75 treatment interviews with the psychiatrist)	Boston	37 per cent
	New Haven	31 per cent
	Detroit	25 per cent

TREATMENT FOR FAMILIES

Medical care provided	Boston	12 per cent
	New Haven	25 per cent
	Detroit	33 per cent

The Treatment Program

		Approximate figures
Economic aid secured	Boston	12 per cent
	New Haven	25 per cent
	Detroit	33 per cent
Educational and social contacts made	Boston	90 per cent
	New Haven	87 per cent
	Detroit	96 per cent

Families with whom no treatment undertaken after first study of case:

Father psychotic, mother paranoid	1
Parents dull, attitude hopeless	2
Mother dead, stepfather dissolute	1
	4

Psychiatric treatment not indicated because no present emotional difficulties, but services when needed rendered family in other ways   13

Parents, in particular the responsible parent or substitute, early found impossible to work with from psychiatric standpoint, though services rendered family in other ways:

Psychotic or abnormal personality or too alcoholic	4
Obstinate rejection of delinquent	2
Too old and ignorant	1
Obstinate protection of delinquent	1
Totally unconcerned	1
	9

Families for whom psychiatric treatment indicated and attempted for various lengths of time but essentially unaccepted—though willing to receive other services:

Parent too dull or ignorant	11
Parent too old or inflexible	2
Parent psychotic	1
Parent abnormal personality	11

Parent not willing to have own behavior (immorality, etc.) disturbed	12
Parent too strongly confronted with own difficulties in life situation	7
Parent not willing to recognize own failures	4
Parent jealous of authority, resented outside interference	2
	50
Families accepting psychiatric treatment on more surface levels of emotional relationships—otherwise treatment largely educational	41
Families with whom deeper treatment of emotional relationships attempted (this includes some of the most heavily delinquent cases and some of the most involved emotional relationships)	26
	143

MODIFICATION OF PARENT BY TREATMENT ON ANY LEVEL

In 123 cases where attitude of parent clearly was involved in delinquent's problem and treatment was attempted

Parent not essentially modified even though first responses to treatment were favorable (58 cases)	Boston	33	per cent
	New Haven	57	per cent
	Detroit	53	per cent
Parent somewhat modified in attitudes and behavior toward delinquent (28 cases)	Boston	30	per cent
	New Haven	21.5	per cent
	Detroit	16	per cent
Parent much modified in attitudes and behavior toward delinquent (37 cases)	Boston	37	per cent
	New Haven	21.5	per cent
	Detroit	31	per cent

Modification of parent accepting psychiatric treatment
    Treatment accepted on more surface levels of emotional relationships (41 cases)
        Parent not modified   4 cases

The Treatment Program

Parent somewhat modified	14 cases
Parent much modified	23 cases

Treatment attempted on deeper levels of emotional relationships (this includes some of the most difficult cases) (26 cases)

Parent not modified	6 cases
Parent somewhat modified	7 cases
Parent much modified	13 cases

CHAPTER XI

OUTCOMES AND NEW ORIENTATIONS FOR TREATMENT

THE accumulation of publications showing the huge percentages of failure to check delinquent careers by treatment under the law, and the vast importance of the whole problem of delinquency and crime naturally create an immediate interest in the outcome results of this present attempt at intensive treatment for delinquents.[1] With all the necessitated shortening of the research project there still is much to learn from it.

While the original plan called for treatment of the cases over a longer period, yet the time limitations that were eventually enforced permitted programs to be put into action whereby many needs could be met—social, recreational, educational, medical, psychotherapeutic. In each of the three units there was a skilled staff; only a small case load was required to be carried; the family rather than the delinquent was the unit worked with. The procedure of the modern child guidance clinic was adopted and in most instances over a considerable period services of many kinds were rendered fathers, mothers, other members of the family, as well as the delinquents. With this rich treatment program as a back-

1. For the most painstaking evaluation of outcomes in terms of delinquency see especially *Five Hundred Criminal Careers* and *One Thousand Juvenile Delinquents* by S. and E. T. Glueck, and our own earlier publication, *Delinquents and Criminals; Their Making and Unmaking*. We know very well that these studies and our present evaluations pay little attention to increased severity or, on the other hand, to relative mildness or infrequency of subsequent delinquencies. Nor are other gains in personality development or better adjustments to school, work, etc., credited. Such evaluations as are utilized in the Smith College School of Social Work studies of outcomes of guidance clinic cases are more satisfactory, but we have thought it advisable in this report of outcomes to stress continuance in or cessation from delinquency as the main fact at issue.

ground, we have made a most careful evaluation of what was accomplished for the prevention of delinquency in terms of the cases with which we worked. Incidental results accruing from parental education and from promoting the welfare of different members of the family, even as these have a bearing upon prevention of delinquency in the younger children, we have not attempted to estimate.

To give any statement of massed figures of cessation or continuance of delinquency is meaningless and offers no basis for betterment of practical procedure. Indeed the adding together of all sorts of cases to form a total may have a harmful effect upon sound thinking about delinquency because it implies that delinquents form a homogeneous group with equal possibilities of being successfully treated. Any statements that tend to preserve prevalent erroneous generalizations about the causes of delinquency and that perpetuate the commonly held false theories about the possibilities of uniform treatment of delinquents form great barriers to progress.

Delinquency is a symptom, a symptom of some personal or social maladjustment, and its rational treatment should be analogous to therapy in medical science. Such a symptom as fever is regarded as evidence of some pathological process which requires diagnosis and is to be treated according to the special reactions exhibited by the patient. To carry the analogy a step further, it would be absurd for a hospital or a clinic to produce statistics about whether patients with fever did or did not get well. It would be equally uninstructive and senseless for us to sum up in one total all the cases that have ceased from or have continued in delinquency after our attempts at treatment.

New orientations about the possibilities of treatment as learned from rational evaluations of outcomes are very much needed at this stage of our understandings of delinquents and delinquency, and our figures about outcomes are directed toward bringing out some better points of view. Instead of giving "raw scores" of the total number of successes and failures we endeavor to correlate the facts concerning outcomes[2] with our knowledge of the peculiarities, including the established reactive tendencies, of the delinquent and of the environmental situations found possible or impossible to modify. Naturally we cannot in every case answer why there was success or failure but the new orientations which we present go far toward that desirable end.

Appreciation of how greatly the figures on outcomes prove the validity of our new orientation demands a clear grasp of the practical issues which are involved in treatment possibilities. So first of all we present the facts underlying certain groupings of cases, the groups representing special needs of the delinquent and potentialities for treatment. To bring these matters into focus, we have attempted to formulate with as sharp differentiation as our present knowledge allows the nuclear issues which are necessary to be met if there is to be advance in the treatment of delinquents. While these groupings were not altogether new to our thought, our present conceptions of them are based on very careful consideration of the data provided by this present study. Moreover our ideas about the preëminent importance of certain types of facts concerning delinquents have been confirmed through the opportunity which this research has afforded for experimentation in treatment. We did not allow any preconceptions to interfere with ardent attempts at therapy, even in the instances where our earlier experience would have led us to prognosticate failure by any methods of treatment which under existing conditions we could put into operation. And it should go without saying that we could even more easily foresee continued failure in the same cases from juvenile

2. Information concerning the careers of our cases during the two or more years since the clinical units were disbanded has been obtained through recent home visits and by court, probation, police, parole and school records. We believe they are complete and accurate.

court and probationary procedures and, for that matter, even if there were commitments to correctional institutions as now organized. Our goal was to undertake vigorous attempts at therapy with all types of delinquents and families, in order to ascertain what sorts of conditions or situations within or external to the individual are or are not insuperable obstacles to skilled treatment service.

The new orientation which seeks to incorporate in as few categories as possible some prognostic criteria extremely significant for determination of treatment plans and possibilities leads to these primary groupings:

GROUP I

In one group we may classify all those delinquents who cannot be considered hopeful for treatment under even ordinarily good conditions of family and community life. They are the abnormal or the markedly neurotic personalities, or those suffering from severe mental conflicts, and mental defectives—any of these who have already established delinquent tendencies. The weak powers of resistance or the special inner stresses of such delinquents cause them readily to give way to impulses and hence it is very unlikely that they will respond to treatment sufficiently to refrain from delinquency, unless they are in a controlled environment free from ordinary incitements to delinquency.

Except perhaps for certain mental conflict cases, we are considering in this grouping the pathological nature of the delinquent himself rather than his aberrant behavior. And here we may well remember that a great master of medicine used to say that very frequently it is far less important to know what disease a man has than it is to recognize what sort of a man has the disease.

The phenomenon of delinquency as it appears in the cases of Group I has exactly the same genetic implications as in all other cases. The delinquency of a neurotic or abnormal personality, for example, arises from thwartings or other obstructions to urges, desires, and wishes, and represents activities leading off into the current of search for substitute satisfactions. The specific delinquency also represents some specific type of reactive behavior—as formulated in Chapter IX. But the possibility of effective treatment, the prognosis, in these cases is mainly dependent upon the personality characteristics and disorders that differentiate the group.

First, concerning mentally defective delinquents: it should be well understood that any main division of delinquents in terms of normal intelligence versus mental defect is an oversimplified procedure to be swept aside as of very little value. Given simple surroundings, good training, and an environment which does not especially incite to delinquency, on the average the mental defective is little or no more susceptible to becoming delinquent than are others. Or taken in hand early as a delinquent and afforded treatment according to his obvious needs, institutional or otherwise environmental, he is equally as reformable as the common run of delinquents of good mental ability.[3] Later, when there are confirmed delinquent trends, the protection of society may, of course, require permanent custodial care of the defective individual. But defectives do not constitute a homogeneous group; this is as true of personality characteristics as it is of mental age levels. Researches conducted and published earlier by ourselves and others indicate that successful early treatment of defectives who have become delinquent depends more largely on favorable personality characteristics than on any other factor.[4] All this appeared so definitely estab-

3. E. H. Sutherland has made a particularly well-balanced study of the relation of mental defect to delinquency and crime. He concludes that as a *general factor* it is relatively unimportant. See *Principles of Criminology*, 1934, p. 95, or his original study, "Mental Deficiency and Crime," Chapter XV in *Social Attitudes*, edited by Kimball Young, 1931.

4. See "Follow-up Studies of Mental Defectives," A. F. Bronner, *Proceedings American Association on Mental Deficiency*, 1933; and "A Study

lished that no purpose seemed to be served in accepting mental defectives and their families for treatment in this research project.

For inclusion in Group I there should be considered, aside from defective delinquents, those who, if showing severe delinquent tendencies can be definitely diagnosed as abnormal personalities of various types, brain injury cases, post-encephalitics, confirmed homosexuals, psychotics or pre-psychotics, as well as severe cases of neurosis and the "neurotic characters" who through the irrational nature of their delinquencies give evidence of suffering from severe mental conflicts.

Among our 143 delinquents we considered 26 cases properly to be classified as belonging to this group. (Through incomplete early diagnosis one defective was included.) This 18 per cent of the cases may or may not represent the proportion to be found in any ordinary "run-of-the-mill," but it is our guess from past experience that if confirmed delinquent defectives were included not far from 20 per cent of delinquents in any unselected series would properly belong in Group I. We believe this because we have been very cautious in making this diagnostic and prognostic classification and probably leaned over backwards somewhat in order not to introduce unwarranted pathological considerations.

These 26 delinquents had all been troublesome members of society, indeed at least 10 of them had already exhibited rather costly careers. Most of them were recidivists and their arrests and appearances in court would make a remarkable total; 6 had been in correctional institutions. A conspicious feature in their histories was the routine character of the efforts to control their delinquent tendencies. That they belonged to any prognostic classification had been unrecog-

of Recidivists and First Offenders of Average and Defective Intelligence," M. E. Shimberg and J. Israelite, *American Journal of Orthopsychiatry*, April, 1933.

nized, important as this was from the standpoint of efficient disposition of the case; that the ordinary methods of handling them had led to no improvement had constituted no challenge to undertaking special studies of why this was so. Measures had not been carried out for special segregation or for thoroughgoing treatment, nor had the protection of society been well considered. In nearly every instance the essential nature of the individual who was being dealt with was not taken into account—which implies that society's provisions for dealing with delinquents who fall in this grouping are to be regarded in general as weak, unscientific, and noneducative for the offender and for those charged with responsibility for his reform.

It required no long investigation on our part to diagnose the problems which 24 of these youthful offenders presented in their own nature or in their internal difficulties, and the other 2 were classified after a short amount of work with them. From our earlier experiences with such types of cases we might have recognized the likelihood that little or nothing could be accomplished by working with them under the ordinary conditions of community life. But since we had our great opportunity for experimental therapeutic research and since it seemed certain that routine methods of treatment would entail only further failure and further cost to society, we felt justified in utilizing a great amount and variety of therapeutic endeavor, if only as experimentation. (Details of treatment for special cases as related to outcomes appear in the next chapter.) What were the results?

For the 26 cases in Group I it appears that only one individual at the end of the treatment period had overcome his delinquent tendencies—and even he later got into more trouble. Three others were rated as much improved, but likewise did not retain their improvement.

Our follow-up investigations which cover at least two sub-

sequent years[5] show that of the total only 5 cases are reported as having been doing positively well during this period—and we confess lack of complete confidence in the future for all of these.

The chiefly negative results of our treatment research as applied to this group of cases amply prove the main point, namely, the need for orienting classification. An immense saving of futile effort will be possible through such a prognostic grouping based on scientifically conducted studies. The protection of society and the establishment of any adequate attempts at reforming delinquents classified in Group I call for highly specialized treatment, indeed experimental reëducational procedures, with provisions for long-time segregation and, in some cases, for prolonged psychotherapy while the delinquent is hospitalized, as it were, in some colony or home.

The diagnostic classification of the cases in Group I is as follows:

GROUP I

	Cases
Neurotic or psychoneurotic	9
Traumatic personality—brain injury cases	3
Abnormal personality	
Egocentric unstable personality	2
Epileptic personality	1
Unclassified abnormal personality	1
Mildly psychotic or "pre-psychotic"	4
Homosexual personality	1
Defective delinquent	1
Severe mental conflicts	4
	26

[5]. This minimum period really applies only to the Detroit cases where the research unit disbanded in 1933; in New Haven the follow-up period represents three years; at the present writing the Boston cases have been known for four years since the clinic closed.

GROUP II

As belonging to a second group there should be placed all those cases in which the social pathology, particularly as involving human relationships within or outside the family circle, appears to weigh so heavily against the possibility of successful treatment of the delinquent in his family environment that the given situation seems largely hopeless. These cases present facts so obvious that the prognostic implications should in all common sense be clearly recognized in order that there may be economy of effort on the part of those who deal with delinquents, that society may be better protected, that more radical and possibly reconstructive measures may be carried out.

A certain amount of subjective judgment is involved in grouping a small percentage of these cases, but here as for the other groups the nuclear issues are clear; it is only the exceptional cases about which there is much doubt. It has required comparatively little investigation, such as our psychiatric social workers made, to come to a well-founded decision about the probabilities of success or failure of treatment in the given situation. It required more than a bare enumeration of environmental data; requisite also, we found, was the weighing of social relationships as they had been affecting or were likely to affect the delinquent. Then, the delinquent's own personality had to be taken into account especially as related to the possibility of his gaining insight, strength, and independence to be able to become immune to the social pathology. This comes out clearly when we note that by no means all of the 131 delinquents who were found to be living under inimical conditions (see Chapter III) are included in Group II. The point is that not only the kind and the quantity of the existing social pathology, but also the dynamic values which such pathology has for the particular personality of the delinquent have to be considered in the prognosis.

We classified 50 cases as belonging to Group II. To show in part at least the kinds of social pathology which existed in these 50 cases and which were large factors in leading us to form the judgment that treatment of the delinquent would be hopeless if he remained at home and that the social pathology could not be speedily remedied we offer the following data. In the family life of this group the main social pathology, leaving aside combinations of liabilities, was as follows :-

Psychosis including alcoholic psychosis	7 parents
Severely alcoholic	8 parents
Abnormal personalities or severely psychoneurotic	9 parents
Definitely immoral	7 parents
Mentally defective	5 parents
Criminalistic	3 parents
Dire poverty	1 family
Main social pathology in relationships outside the family circle	10 families

With regard to the last item it should be stated that no less than 80 per cent of the families in Group II lived in high delinquency areas, although in only 20 per cent was this considered to be the main factor in the social pathology. With such social relationships as these existing for the young individual it would seem to be plain why we classified the cases as belonging to Group II. But then at once arises the question: why in these same families and under the same neighborhood conditions were some of the children non-delinquent? Since we have discussed this matter at length in the chapters which compare delinquents and controls, we need here only reiterate that immense differences were found between the delinquent and non-delinquent in deeply-felt thwartings, deprivations, inferiorities and other emotional discomforts versus very little or no such essential unhappinesses. Delinquency represented the search for compensatory satisfactions; the non-delinquent was able to find satisfactions that counterbalanced whatever adversity was sensed in the environment.

Our judgment that nothing could be accomplished without radical modification of the delinquent's life situation did not lead us, any more than with the personality problems of Group I, to refrain from carrying out a complete therapeutic program. Our research included the project Of working with families even if early investigations showed them to be very difficult, in order to demonstrate what skilled effort could or could not accomplish when environmental conditions weighed so heavily against the delinquent's chances of being reformed that such effort did not seem hopeful. Leaving the details for the next chapter, the real story of what we were able or not able to accomplish in this segment of the total treated cases—the 35 per cent where the social pathology was stacked so greatly against us—runs as follows:

At the end of the treatment period 16 of the cases had ceased being delinquent and at the end of the follow-up period of more than two years 10 of these had certainly held their gains.

The final report is that 19 cases (38 per cent) of Group II have not been delinquent during a period of two or more years.

Concerning this final report it should at once be stated that in 11 instances the delinquent was removed from home —4 were among those sent to institutions and 7 went to foster homes. Analysis of the probable reasons for the unexpected success so far of the 8 cases remaining with their families appears in the next chapter.

In 7 other cases not rated as completely non-delinquent during the follow-up period very marked improvement is noted. Almost all of these have no further court appearances; where this has occurred it is for very minor offenses—and of these cases later.

This leaves 23 (46 per cent) of the cases in Group II who have definitely continued to be delinquent—8 of these are now in correctional institutions.

That the great amount of work done with some of these cases and their families had quite a measure of success does not militate against the correctness of their having been classified in Group II. Besides removal of the child from home, much work was undertaken in many instances that would be difficult to duplicate without our exceptional equipment, opportunities, and backing; and it would be hard to tell how much influence even shorter contacts had upon delinquents and their families.

In the face of these facts there can be no question of the value of considering in one special group all those cases which proved to have severe social pathology in the background, especially such human relationships as give little promise of alteration for the better and weight the scales heavily against the chances of reconstructing the delinquent's behavior.

GROUP III

THIS group of 67 consisted of cases in which after thorough investigation or earliest attempts at treatment, the outcome seemed hopeful. They were individuals whose personality or internal difficulties did not show extreme deviations and they came from conditions where the social pathology did not give evidences of greatly weighing against chances of successful treatment. This does not mean that the cases were less severely delinquent or that none exhibited any signs of abnormality, neuroticism, and conflict; nor does it mean that there was no social pathology, as witness our findings for the whole series of cases as given on page 29, but rather that the factors of personality difficulty and social pathology were not so severe or so piled up that they seemed to offer insuperable obstacles to therapy.

Thus in Group III, though there were 8 severely alcoholic parents, 2 defective and 2 with criminal records, we almost invariably found, in contrast to the families of Group II, counteracting social assets. Then, while for the 80 per cent in Group II who lived in high delinquency areas we could find no offsetting resources in family relationships, the 36 per cent in Group III who were confronted with similarly inimical environmental conditions had other relatively favorable situations in family life.

Group III obviously comprises the cases with whom there should have been the highest percentage of success—and the outcomes corroborated our expectations. Beyond giving the results, little need be said at this point—the type of modifications found possible and the blockings to treatment are best stated in correlating the case outcomes with the treatment attempted. Then in this group it is our failures rather than the favorable response to our manifold therapeutic efforts that need explanation. The outcomes for Group III are as follows:

At the end of the treatment period 55 of the cases had ceased delinquency, but for this group where it was possible to gain more ready response and coöperation than in the other groups the results while treatment was going on are not nearly so significant as the after-effects.

During the follow-up period of two years or more, 48 cases (72 per cent) of Group III have not been delinquent. As a matter of fact, 43 of these successful cases have been non-delinquent for considerably more than two years—they had ceased being offenders long before the clinic treatment stopped, which in Boston and New Haven is already three and a half years ago.

Justification for this third grouping seems as clear as for the other groups. The prognostic possibilities of treatment are proven by the much greater proportion of successes. Evidently it is of great value to undertake sound appraisals in terms of whether or not therapeutic effort will be an economical procedure if the delinquent remains in the family circle. (Only 5 of this group—7.5 per cent as compared to 38 per cent of Group II—were placed in foster homes.) The better results for this group were not due to relatively greater efforts on our part, made because the cases appeared more promising. As we have earlier emphasized, the research aspects of our project very frequently led us to undertake the most intensive work with the most difficult cases—and these included many of the cases in the other groups. Thus from every side we are forced to appreciate the worth of prognostic orientation.

THIS presentation of prognostic orientations as related to the results of treatment may well end with a comparative statement of outcomes for the three groups.

COMPARISON OF OUTCOMES

	Groups		
	I	II	III
During treatment period			
Delinquency ceased	1	16	55
Much improved though some minor delinquencies	3	11	3
Delinquencies continued	22	23	9
	26	50	67
During two years or more since treatment period			
Non-delinquent	5 (19%)	19 (38%)	48 (72%)
Remaining in institution since treatment period or on parole less than 2 years	2	..	..
Much improvement: rare minor delinquency	3	7	5

	Groups		
	I	II	III
Delinquency continued	15 (58%)	23 (46%)	13 (19%)
Dead	..	1	..
Whereabouts unknown	..	..	1
Migratory; probably doing well as judged by occasional reports	1	..	..
	26	50	67
During treatment period in institutions	14	11	5
During treatment period in foster homes	8	19	5
Now in institutions or recently on parole	13	8	1
Remaining in foster homes	2	9	1

CHAPTER XII

OUTCOMES CORRELATED WITH TREATMENT

HERE the more significant facts related to the specific treatment of delinquents and to outcomes are discussed under the diagnostic and prognostic grouping system of the preceding chapter.

GROUP I

THOUGH it seems clear that the 26 delinquents in Group I required very special consideration for treatment removed from the community, yet this does not mean that every case of abnormal personality, neuroticism, or severe mental conflict demands segregation. The criteria for making the distinction are mainly based on the severity of the personality deviation or of the neurosis, and on the extent to which delinquency represents an habitual form of behavior. Then, of course, the family relationships and the total environment have to be taken into account in all cases, especially with neurotics.

The delinquents with personality deviations in Group I do not quite coincide with the figures for such cases as given in Chapter IV: two constitutional inferior personalities apparently merely needed simpler living conditions, one encephalitis case and one schizoid personality appeared to be improvable.

Then, concerning the neurotics we note that 9 were placed in Group I, and 10 were not. (It became evident through later comparison of the cases that at least in one instance we misjudged the original facts—as we see it now this case also should have been considered as hopeless for treatment in the community.) The matter is worth dwelling on because discriminations are involved, the validity of which is of interest to professional workers in this field. Those who were classified in Group I were older, with longer records of delinquency, with one exception they showed more signs of neuroticism, and in these instances there were more difficult family emotional situations with which to contend, indeed in 4 cases there were parents who were themselves abnormal.

Furthermore, aside from classification of the delinquent as neurotic or as an abnormal personality, we placed in Group I four delinquents who were experiencing deep-seated mental conflicts growing out of family relationships and which certainly required prolonged psychiatric treatment away from the family situation.

Profiting by earlier experience with such types of cases, we might have recommended prolonged institutional care for at least 17 of the delinquents save for the fact of the difficulties encountered in legally detaining them for a period of years; and then we knew well that there was little likelihood of their receiving any scientifically directed treatment. Six of them had already been in institutions with little benefit resulting except temporary protection of society. Not that we more than anyone else could have prescribed the kinds of therapeutic effort which would bring about fundamental changes in their conduct tendencies, nor could we have said how long these cases should be detained. But we did know that professional effort under legally imposed and properly controlled conditions, experimental though this effort might be in spirit and character, should be directed toward solving these very difficult social and personal problems. Without the experimental attack we shall know no more in the future than we do now about what to do with such cases as form this group.

For 8 more of the delinquents, including the ones suffering from deep mental conflicts, we saw that long-continued psychotherapy was essential and that this properly should be undertaken with the individual removed from the disturbing conditions of family life and other emotion provoking situations.

Frankly we did not know what could be done to modify the homosexual tendencies of the one other delinquent—twin case D. Nothing that can be practically carried out is known to be curative. We believed that this boy's non-sexual delinquent tendencies might be bettered through treatment aimed at them, and this proved to be so.

Our treatment program for this group included the following: Intensive psychotherapy was attempted with 15 delinquents, a much greater proportion than in either of the other groups; recreational and educational adjustments were made; 8 were found foster homes where contact could be kept with them. In all but two cases, where nothing could even be attempted, the families were worked with to the best of our ability—mainly in the endeavor to educate them in understanding the nature and needs of the delinquent. In only 5 cases would the parents accept treatment on a psychiatric level for betterment of their emotional attitudes toward the delinquent, but then we discovered that in 8 instances there were parents who were themselves in some respects abnormal. The immediate response of parents was often favorable enough, but our estimation of their modification in terms of what we deemed necessary—although perhaps we cannot fairly make too much of this point, since the troubles of the delinquents were so largely within themselves —was that in only one case were the parents much modified, though somewhat altered in attitudes in five other instances.

Finding that so little could be accomplished, we were more than willing that 14 of these delinquents should be sent to institutions during the treatment period—although in only the case which was rapidly developing a psychosis and in another who was sent to a custodial institution for long-time care did we think that an adequate program of treatment was being planned.

Our follow-up investigations which covered at least two years and in most cases three years show that 7 of the 26 delinquents in Group I are in institutions. They had been committed or recommitted since our clinic ceased being active, but only the 2 mentioned above are where they are likely to be detained for long periods. Four others are on parole and 3 are in foster homes.

Considering the peculiarities exhibited by those in this Group we have much curiosity about the reasons *why even 5 have been able to do well during these subsequent years*—the 5 that were mentioned in the last chapter, 2 of them neurotics.

ONE boy who was reacting by very violent antisocial behavior to his conflicts about his family relationships was given much friendliness, recognition, and psychiatric help before and after an institutional commitment. Then his parents were considerably changed in their attitudes through efforts of social workers. The boy stabilized greatly and evidently largely resolved his conflicts by gaining insight into the real causes of his own earlier delinquencies.

ANOTHER boy from a very decent family with hard working parents had terrific emotional disturbances, the nature of which we never completely solved. At fourteen years he had some seven years of delinquency behind him and already had seven appearances in the juvenile court. To what extent he was modified by the comparatively small amount of work we were able to do with him is hard to say, but somehow our contacts with him and his family played some part in the results. His delinquency which appeared to be on the basis of a compulsion neurosis completely ceased, but then he became an entirely different type of problem. His parents acquired a farm; he went out to live on it and has become a very repressed, withdrawn young fellow, overquiet and distinctly needing treatment from the standpoint of his mental health.

Treatment and Outcomes 177

THE mentally defective boy whom we inadvertently included in our cases for treatment has ceased to be delinquent. After we made the diagnosis no custodial care was forthcoming, but the boy was removed from his miserable family conditions and placed in a very simple country foster home where he was well-accepted. He has been doing well.

WHEN the girl whose personality characteristics and history of earlier attacks led us to make a diagnosis of epileptic personality was during the treatment period placed in a foster home, she continued to be delinquent; then for a short time she was in an institution. Realizing that her behavior largely represented reactions to unsatisfactory family relationships and poor parental example, we took on her epileptic father and unreasonable mother for reëducative treatment while the girl was away. The home life and family attitudes became much improved and the girl after returning to her parents was not further delinquent.

A BOY of sixteen was heavily delinquent as a reaction to a most extraordinary family situation. On the one hand, it was a repressively overreligious household and, at the other extreme, promiscuous sexual relationships prevailed among old and young. The boy was experiencing a tremendous emotional conflict about all this and had a deep sense of guilt about his own part in the affairs as well as about his other delinquencies. Though re-educative and psychiatric therapy was undertaken, the boy and his family could not be modified rapidly enough and he had to be sent to an institution. (This was the family where the two sisters reacted by ardently desiring to become missionaries.) Our work with the family was continued and with some success. When paroled the boy returned home, became greatly interested as he had never been before in the church and its activities, obtained work, married, and for more than two years has maintained a thoroughly good record.

EVEN from these stories of accomplishment it is rather easy to see why we have some skeptical reservations about the future for at least some of these few cases of Group I which have done well during the follow-up period.

GROUP II

For the 50 delinquents of Group II, those where the social pathology was heavily weighted against successful treatment, the specific treatment undertaken and the correlated results for the follow-up period of two years or more may be summarized as follows:

Foster-home placement during treatment period—19 cases

Non-delinquent during follow-up period   8
- Remaining in foster homes   3
- Returned to modified parents   3
- Returned to changed home conditions   1
- Delinquent in foster homes, then institution, long parole supervision, still great risk   1

Much improved during follow-up period   5
- Remaining in foster homes   4
- Returned home when old enough to work and have independence from paranoid father   1

Delinquency continued   6
- Remaining in foster home though occasionally delinquent   2
- Delinquent in foster home and sent to correctional institution   1
- Did well in foster home but returned to unmodified parents and delinquency recurred   3

To correctional institution during treatment period—11 cases
(Two previously in foster homes, as above)

Non-delinquent during follow-up period   4
- Long parole supervision, somewhat better home conditions, still great risk   1
- Returned to modified parents   1
- Independence through working and living away from bad family   1
- Working, new satisfactions   1

Much improved during follow-up period   1
- Returned to father who separated from dissolute mother   1

Treatment and Outcomes 179

Delinquency continued 5
- Returned to unsatisfying home life, renewal of delinquent associations 2
- Returned to very bad home conditions 2
- Did well for 2 years, then arrested, but some question of guilt 1

Dead 1

Remained at home—in many instances against advice—22 cases

A. Much treatment actually done in attempt to meet difficulties—14 cases

Non-delinquent during follow-up period 4
- Separated parents reunited, home conditions better 1
- Ceased delinquent associations and became seclusive and repressed 1
- When older earned and independent 1
- Family attitudes improved 1

Much improved during follow-up period 1
- Impossible to modify parents, boy was helped—still risk 1

Delinquency continued 9
- Did well under close supervision, but family situation essentially unchanged 5
- Never did well; social pathology irremediable 1
- Neurotic—treatment unavailing 1
- Constitutional inferior personality—suitable environment never found 1
- Did well under close supervision—later gangster activities 1

B. Treatment attempted but less done due to various blockings—8 cases

Non-delinquent during follow-up period 4
- Poverty alleviated 2
- Became conscience-stricken as grew older 1
- Cause unknown 1

Delinquency continued 4
- Parents not modifiable—children continued immersed in delinquency 4

SINCE the social pathology was so much implicated in this group of cases, intensive psychiatric work with the delinquent appeared less important in most instances than more radical procedures to change the environmental conditions. Yet in 11 instances such intensive treatment was undertaken and sometimes together with foster-home placement. Naturally, placement away from home was advocated and carried out for the members of this group much more often than for the other groups.

Psychiatric treatment with the parents, as might be expected, was rejected or otherwise found quite impossible with a large number of the families, 32 of them, while such type of treatment was undertaken with parents in 16 families. Our final estimation was that in only 5 families did the parents appear much modified in their behavior or attitudes, while 7 were somewhat modified.

Considering all this and our early prognosis, it seems that to have 38 per cent of the delinquents in this group free from delinquency during two or more years of the follow-up period is a surprisingly good result. Then 7 more certainly showed vast improvement in behavior. It is clearly impossible to estimate in many cases just what was accomplished by our contacts and our treatment—sometimes perhaps more than we knew and often more than we anticipated could be accomplished. Here again we must emphasize that in extent and intensity the services that we rendered were much greater than could be expected from a probation officer or from an ordinary clinic.

Frequently unfortunate obstructions were met. For example, we often regretted that after foster home placement or institutional life a delinquent had to return to a home with the social pathology largely or entirely unaltered. All clinical observers inveigh against this; it represents so much essentially wasted effort since so many cases then revert to their delinquent trends.

In the above tabular statement of correlations of outcomes with treatment, we have given some indication why the individual did well or poorly after the treatment period. *There remains special interest in the fact that 8 who remained at home have done so well.* The facts are partly given above but there is something to add about a few of them.

ONE boy of 15 when we began work with him had been for seven years a delinquent. During the treatment period, recognition by the clinic and satisfactions accruing through educational plans adapted to his abilities and interests were apparently the cause of cessation of delinquency. At a last inquiry when he was 19 years old he states that his increasing love for his frail mother, his feeling of responsibility toward her, and his fear of being committed have made him refrain from delinquency. We suspect also that his satisfactory employment for a year or more has had something to do with it.

ANOTHER boy who ceased delinquency after years of being a very active offender became, like the case in Group I, very repressed and seclusive. He avoids all companionship except that of his protective, non-delinquent brother and, unoccupied, stays much at home with his mother. Very evidently he has changed from a behavior to a mental health problem.

Two delinquent brothers in the same family seemed to have no conscience about stealing; the family was very poor, frequently evicted, and the parents undoubtedly connived by receiving the goods that these small boys brought home. Perhaps through the alleviation of their poverty both parents and children have altered their attitudes, for the reports about the boys have been very satisfactory.

IN one case the cause of the cessation of delinquency is quite unknown. It may be that the abnormal, paranoid father who refused to coöperate with us strenuously undertook to control his delinquent son, since the boy has no further record.

OF the 24 in Group II who have been definitely delinquent during the past two or more years, 8 are now in correctional institutions and one was in jail awaiting trial when last we heard. In 20 instances the delinquent either remained at home or was returned from foster homes or institutions to his home—in all these we estimated that the parents and homes were essentially unmodified by any treatment that we had offered. Making the same point in another way, we may state that in only 4 instances among these failures did we feel that we had modified the social pathology to any appreciable extent whatever.

GROUP III

THE thoroughly good results obtained with 48 delinquents, namely, 72 per cent of those in Group III, were unquestionably largely due to coöperation of the parents with us. It was found possible with them to establish a psychiatric treatment relationship in 43 instances. Our final estimation was that in 28 cases this resulted in much modification of parental attitudes and behavior, and that in only 2 was there no modification at all. These families that responded so well showed by far the greatest proportion of successes. To this statement we may add the fact that when, as in 16 cases, intensive psychiatric treatment was done with the delinquent at the same time that the parents were responding to the psychiatric approach, virtually no delinquency recurred during the follow-up period. Only one of these cases is not rated as altogether a success; though in contrast to many earlier offenses he has no court record, we know that he has not been upright in some transactions.

In our treatment efforts with the other 24 families the psychiatric approach seemed either not indicated, or was decided to be impossible, or was rejected by the parents themselves. But of course much else was done, including more surface attempts to re-educate the parents concerning the needs of the children. In 11 families where we knew that the parental behavior and emotional attitudes were involved and the best treatment would have been to give them insight into the nature of the underlying difficulties, our psychiatric efforts were blocked. Though we tried to help these 11 families and the delinquents themselves in other ways the follow-up reports show 5 cases continuing in delinquency, with improvement in 2 other instances. Thus our negative as well as our positive results show the importance of family emotional relationships as factors tending not only to produce delinquent behavior, but also to be reckoned with in the achievement possibilities of treatment.

For the 5 delinquents in this group designated as much improved, it is as true as for those in Group II that there was marked betterment—even the 3 who had been in court at all have appeared for very minor offenses as compared with their former delinquencies.

A major question for discussion in connection with this group is why our treatment efforts failed in any cases. Just as we pondered over the reasons for cessation of delinquency in the other groups, so here we would review the causes for continuance in or recurrence of delinquency in 13 cases. In general it cannot be attributed to lack of effort with the family, for even among these 13 we considered the parental attitude to be much or somewhat modified in 7 instances, though this had little or no effect upon two of the delinquents even during the treatment period. Much work was undertaken with all of the delinquents except one who was speedily sent to an institution. But upon survey of these cases we are surprised to find that, while rich educational and recreational programs were carried out with many, in no one of the failures was intensive psychiatric work with the delinquent undertaken. The response to our work with parents and children was shown in the fact that while our treatment was continued 6 of these 13 cases entirely ceased delinquency and one was much improved. To be certain about what new factors may possibly have arisen to bring about the later misconduct would, of course, require a re-study of every case, but significant interpretations are possible from the case records as they stand.

In the light of facts later obtained it appears that one delinquent should never have been included in this group. His mother, while accenting the religiosity of herself and her side of the family, managed to keep from us and the juvenile court officials the continuing criminalism of three members of the household. Probably we were at fault in not digging up these facts, but they were shrewdly concealed. The boy was a failure during treatment and later.

Three of the boys during the follow-up period fell into the pitfalls of crowd suggestion. Two of them had been able to avoid these while they received the steady recognition of the clinic staff, but once this crutch was removed it became evident that their socially acceptable ego-satisfactions had not grown strong enough to enable them independently to pursue the path of non-delinquency.

A fifth boy had for years been so immersed in delinquent ideation that all that was offered him met with indifferent response. His attitude, developed through early rejection by the father and a definite sense of inferiority in his family circle, had been accentuated by an institutional record. The values which he gives to his ideas of an easy life and "easy money" have become paramount with him. He has no further court record but we are well aware that he is very clever in avoiding it.

Two are clear-cut cases of overattachment to the mother with a conflict about it.[1] While feeling so dependent upon mother-love for their satisfactions they, at the same time, have resented this in themselves and violently sought independence, utilizing delinquency to prove to themselves that they are not weaklings. They show a very interesting contrast to a number of the control cases who, as we have shown in Chapter VI, accepted dependence without conflict and thereby avoided delinquency.

One of these two cases, a mild and rather soft-looking boy, earlier

[1] For an analytic study of a case where a mother fixation was a large element in forming a long criminal career see, "The Victim of Loyalty" in *Roots of Crime,* Alexander and Healy, 1935.

much spoiled, acknowledged that he was deliberately setting out to be "tough." There was a very kindly stepfather in the household, but the boy evidently could not stand the situation and after some serious delinquencies while we were trying to help him begged the court that he be sent to the correctional institution where his delinquent companions were. There it was noted that his thoughts and conversation turned much to the relationship between himself and his mother. He plainly evidenced his desire to remain her little boy, but hated to think that he was "a sissy," as he earlier had been called. From the institution he returned home where he did well for a few months and then again broke out with a wild criminalistic escapade which brought him into court in two states—once more an affair that seems in utter contradiction to the soft side of his nature. In the two months that we had a chance to work intensively with him before he demanded that he be committed, his conflicting impulses were very clear to us; indeed he almost phrased his inner protest at dependence on his mother's love, but there was not time enough either to take many steps toward resolving his conflict or even to establish for him substitute satisfactions as we had planned.

IN the other case where there was great emotional dependence on the mother our treatment was highly successful for a period of three years before the clinic closed. The mother was re-educated in appreciation of the boy's need for emancipation and came to see that his earlier delinquencies were a gesture of protest against the feeling of dependency. Two years later when he was 18 and long out of work, he felt badly that he was not able to help his mother and started traveling, as so many discontented boys did during the economic depression; but "on the road" he joined other vagrant fellows who broke into a store and was committed for that offense. Very likely it is because he had never developed capacity for being thoroughly independent that after five years of honesty he once more got into trouble.

STILL another boy posed as fearless and "a tough guy" with some of the more active youngsters in his poor neighborhood, in order to compensate for small size and school retardation, caused by illness, about both of which he was sensitive. He was definitely jealous of his younger brother who was larger and not backward in school. Though with his pampering mother he was affectionate and helpful we found that he had many phantasies of criminal exploits. His parents were coöperative with us in planning better recreations and providing better opportunities for the boy to obtain status in his family circle and they moved to another section of the city, in order to break up the boy's association with his gang. This seemed to be all that was necessary to do at the time; all went well during the treatment period and for a time later. But probably we should have gone deeper into his emotional difficulties. There was reversion to delinquency and the boy was committed to an institution. We learn that on being paroled he showed extreme hostility to his family, undoubtedly due to revival of his inferiority and jealousy feelings; he became further delinquent and was returned to the institution. It was the priggish younger brother, our control for the delinquent who said, "I had the courage to refuse to go with bad boys"—evidencing again that ideas of courage connote very different types of behavior according to different preconceptions.

IN one instance it was predicted that the case would go to smash when the sustaining prop of the clinic was removed, and so it proved. Before treatment the boy had a very long record of delinquency which was a rather normal response in a delinquent area to intense dissatisfactions centering about many disharmonies which prevailed in the family circle, including disagreements over discipline; the mother being overindulgent and the father being given to much whipping. During treatment which lasted for sixteen months the parents were superficially much modified in their behavior and the boy responded well to psychiatric treatment, to recreational and other plans made for him. He entirely ceased his delinquencies. But these well-meaning parents who were really fond of their children, though willing to follow specific suggestions, were altogether too immature to grasp principles and, when left alone, to manage their family properly. The boy soon reverted to delinquency. In this family it is interesting to note that the only one of the six children who was not delinquent or on the edge of being so was our control, the model older boy, who was duller, shy, rather effeminate, a day-dreaming "mother's boy" staying closely at home.

THE older brother of the twins "A" presents an instance of a strange father-son relationship, equally as peculiar as that which we have portrayed in our story of the twins. Always partial and devoted to this older boy, largely because he had given his blood to the boy in a transfusion operation a few days after the child was born, the father blocked our most earnest attempts at treatment when he found that our plans involved separation of the boy from him. While he willingly allowed the other delinquent boy, one of the twins, to be placed in a foster home, he indignantly broke off contact with us when we proposed any separation from the boy to whom he was so much attached. Although the child had frequent epileptic attacks until he was four and had shown rather typical behavior tendencies afterwards, we hesitated to denominate him an epileptic personality. He was only eight when we began with the case, and the father's spoiling which we hoped to alter—and did with some success— seemed to play a part in the picture. As time went on the boy proved unmodifiable and we have concluded that he should have been classified in Group I as an abnormal personality.

The delinquent one of the twins in this family, as we describe in a former chapter, was heavily rejected by the peculiar father. He did well while placed in foster home for a considerable period, but the foster mother was a relative and quarreling arose between the families. As a result the foster mother would not keep the boy and he was returned to his parents and to renewed association with the very troublesome older brother. As might have been anticipated they soon were delinquent together again and our last report shows that both were recently sent to an institution.

MARKED improvement during the clinic treatment period occurred in the case of a boy of eleven whose old-world parents were grateful for suggestions. And odd-looking endocrine case, less bright than an older brother, the boy thrived under the recognition which we gave him and which we induced the parents to give; besides this he responded somewhat to medical treatment, and educational and recreational projects afforded substitute satisfactions for the delinquency in which he had previously indulged. But though they were willing to follow specific advice the parents never gained sufficient insight to alter essentially their long-established feelings that the boy was a disappointment and altogether inferior to the other children. Without the constant reminders of the social workers, the parents easily reverted to their earlier attitudes of nagging and over-restriction and without the encouragement of outsiders the boy once more felt discouraged and rebellious. It was quite natural that he should turn again to the old sources of compensation and satisfaction and indulge in much the same behavior that earlier led to his appearance in court.

INTENSIVE efforts with the parents on the part of psychiatric social workers over a period of nine months and many recreational and educational projects carried out with the delinquent brought about extremely good results in one case. Though the boy had a tremendous record of delinquency behind him, all of it stopped under treatment. Particularly as a neurotic boy he had been extremely unhappy at school and at home on account of the inadequate management of the family by his mother, the severe punishments administered by his father, and his own physical frailty as compared to his sister's marked vigor. Living in a neighborhood where there was a high delinquency rate, he readily took to delinquency in early life. Up to the time that the clinic ceased operation we counted the case a remarkable success. For reasons unknown to us, though we might guess that the betterment of the family conditions was not retained, within the last year the boy has again become delinquent and has been committed to an institution.

Is it possible to make generalizations about the 13 failures of Group III? The fact that during treatment 6 of these ceased delinquency and one was greatly improved certainly deceived us into believing that what was done for them was adequate. But as we review them now we are impressed by the fact that the deeper emotional issues were largely neglected. As we stated before, though much else was done for the individuals themselves, none were taken on for intensive psychiatric treatment. Our present analysis of these failures convinces us that the best chances for eradication of the delinquent tendencies in 7 instances would have been through such therapy, if we could have persuaded the family and the delinquent to carry on with it. In one other case our treatment was balked through the boy being speedily committed to an institution, and about the other five we are far from certain that we did the best that could have been done if we had been able to obtain strong backing for what we thought was necessary.

That other considerations have much bearing upon the outcomes we doubt. The failures were not to be differentiated from the others in Group III either by their ages or their intelligence levels. The length of time that they had been delinquent seems to be no factor, since the average period of their prior delinquency was 2.7 years as compared to 2.6 years for the others in Group III. Nor is it altogether a matter of whether or not the family life was alterable, for in 7 of the 13 cases the parents were either much or somewhat modified, which compares favorably with our estimate of the modification of parents for the entire Group III. Then it is not a question of the delinquent's response because in nearly every case that was quite good while we were active in treatment. The main point seems to be that we were dealing in 9 cases with reactions to emotional discomforts that were more likely to recur than we realized and that consequently should have been more fundamentally dealt with in a treatment relationship. The dissatisfactions in the other cases were mainly due to some features of the environmental situation which we were powerless to alter.

Perhaps here the reader should again be reminded that even these cases which we assign to Group III, apparently the most favorable for treatment, were difficult delinquents who equally with the others were from the first regarded as potentially serious offenders.

CHAPTER XIII

OTHER DATA CORRELATED WITH OUTCOMES

IN spite of the clear-cut findings of the previous chapters, it is naturally a question whether other factors may have influenced the possibilities of effective treatment. Previous studies have been confined to more objective factual details and since our material contains these also we should perhaps examine them to see whether or not they play a part in influencing outcome.

Did the intelligence level of the delinquent make any differences in the outcome? We cannot find the slightest evidence that those of higher intelligence rating according to standard age-level scales did relatively better either during the treatment period or subsequently. Though the totals are all too small to have any reliability, yet because of the intensity of treatment the findings are of interest—one might expect that the very bright would profit most by the opportunities offered them. As a matter of fact those having I.Q. of 110 or above did not average as well in outcomes as the total group. The delinquents having I.Q.'s ranging from 90 to 110 and from 80 to 90 did not differ significantly in outcomes from each other. The number of I.Q.'s lower than this is too small to have any value. Taking the total cases it is apparent from the table which follows that outcomes are correlated much more closely with the treatment-group placing than with the intellectual status.

Did the age of the delinquent when treatment began have any bearing on the outcome? We are surprised to find that, contrary to general opinion, the youngest age groups did not show the largest proportion of success and that the preadolescent period, 11 to 13 years, showed the worst outcomes. In this latter period there were also the greatest number of shifts in the status between results at the end of the clinic treatment period and the record for the ensuing two or more years—the extent of this not being shown in the tables. It may well be that the young children of our study represent a very high degree of selection since even at their early age they were severely delinquent. Granted that this is probably true, yet it might have been expected that they would have proved more readily modifiable than the older delinquents. Concerning the older ages, those from 14 years up, it is noteworthy that there was 85 per cent cessation of delinquency for the two follow-up years in Group III and even 44 per cent in Group II. Though our numbers are again too small for any statistical reliability, what they do show is of interest because the younger delinquents were treated with quite as much effort as the older ones. We can scarcely believe that interpretation can fairly involve the matter of maturity, since hardly any of our cases have as yet reached the notorious peak age of incidence of delinquency and crime. On the other hand, independence gained through age, earning, or the acquirement of status and other emancipations made possible through increasing age and especially under our treatment efforts did play a part in a considerable number of cases.

Did the length of time during which the delinquent had been an offender before the treatment began play any part in the outcome? Very unexpectedly we find that long years of delinquency offered no barrier to successful treatment of already or potentially serious offenders. The table shows that the figures in some divisions are so small that many comparisons cannot fairly be made, but the above statement holds true for both Groups II and III. It may be that the figures for longer periods of delinquency have to be interpreted mainly in the light of what we stated above about the older ages; however it is surprising to find that those less than 14 years of age sometimes had been delinquent four or more years. That so many of the cases in Group III had not been delinquent longer than one year is not so surprising since they represent the instances in which the social pathology was not so severe—and the latter fact probably plays a greater part in the successful outcomes than the fact that they were delinquent a comparatively shorter time.

Did the length of time that the clinic had the case under treatment have any relationship to the outcomes? We have asked ourselves this question in order to decide whether the failures may have been slighted cases—and whether the converse is true. Attempts to answer are largely complicated by the great variabilities in the treatment necessitated by attempts to meet exigencies and needs, case by case. It merely seems clear that in some instances a shorter service has proven sufficient and that in Group I the only successes were those who had a long period of treatment. The trouble in making interpretations is enhanced by the fact that it was the special needs of the most difficult cases that seemed to justify the longest efforts. The median term of service as given in the table at the end of the chapter would indicate that most cases in all groups were under treatment for very considerable periods.

Was treatment more successful relatively with those who had appeared in court only once? A thoroughly rational preconception would seem to be that the chances for success with the delinquent would be much greater if treatment were begun shortly after the first court experience. If from our small figures we may derive an answer, it would seem that when the social pathology is great there is little difference in results depending on whether the offender is in court once or more times, but when, as in Group III, the social pathology is less the chance for cessation of delinquency under treatment is much more when the delinquent is in court for the first time. Again here we must remember that a first appearance in court by no means indicates that there has not already been a long career of delinquency; indeed the seven delinquents who had not been in court at all or at the most only informally, but who were referred to us for treatment

Other Data and Outcomes

on account of their delinquency, proved to have been delinquent on the average for three years. We know full well again here that many factors enter into the results, but the main point is that the outcomes appear to be very greatly affected by the amount of social pathology.

Is it probable that the outcomes, or any given proportion of them, would have been as satisfactory if the delinquents had merely remained on probation? We put this question because it very naturally may be raised by someone, but who can answer it with any certitude? In the first place we must leave Group I out of consideration because with any methods and facilities now available outcomes for cases of the types included are very likely to be poor. The totals for Groups II and III show that 54 per cent had already been on probation for varying lengths of time and were recidivists in court. Many of the others who had been only once in court had earlier been in conflict with school authorities and some of them had earlier been arrested but not taken to court. If we put these facts together with the figures for cessation of delinquency (38 per cent in Group II and 72 per cent in Group III), to say nothing of the cases in which there is very marked improvement, and compare them with the findings of the Glueck study in which only 12 per cent had been free from delinquency five years after probation ended, we have very pertinent suggestions of what our treatment may have accomplished.

To what extent did foster home placement prove valuable? It will be seen from the table which follows this chapter that 32 delinquents were placed in foster homes. As might be expected, such placement seemed most imperative for Group II cases. Very little was accomplished by placing 8 delinquents belonging to Group I. Among the other 24 which were placed, 18 have ceased delinquency or shown great improvement. However there are 10 cases remaining and doing well in foster homes; their future behavior undoubtedly depends largely upon the conditions to which they return, if we may judge by the fact that 4 whose delinquencies continued showed much improvement in foster homes but were returned to parents who had proved unmodifiable by our treatment. This contrasts with 7 successes who returned to modified parents.

Is it possible to correlate the success or failure of treatment with alleviation of specific emotional discomforts? Unfortunately the question cannot be answered; it is an important goal for future research. The reader may be reminded that such deep-lying factors were discovered to be related to the causation of delinquency in 92 per cent of the cases. Our reorientations concerning causations of delinquency have been forced upon us only through later thoroughgoing studies of the accumulated material that enabled us to formulate the fundamental issues. During the period of practical work there was no organized attempt to interpret treatment in terms of furnishing the delinquent with needed emotional satisfactions, whether by modifying his immediate social environment or by giving him substitutive satisfactions. Nevertheless it is probably fair to infer that the parents of Group III who responded to treatment were through our efforts enabled to appreciate the emotional difficulties under which the delinquent labored and to make the changes in family life which, at least in some measure, met the needs of the delinquent. But at this stage it is unsafe to attempt evaluations of these deeper issues—our judgments would be highly subjective.

If the delinquent ceases his delinquent activities, does he develop personality problems? We have asked ourselves this question because it has been suggested by some psychiatrists that if delinquency is reactive behavior to emotional discomforts, the shutting off of such outlets will turn the individual's instinctual urges from seeking relief in outer activities to being unhealthily absorbed in inner conflicts. We have been on the look-out for personality disorders as they may result from repression of urges that found a vent in delinquency but have found it only twice in our series, the cases spoken of earlier as now presenting mental hygiene problems. Granting that occasionally there may be this danger where delinquency is the expression of deep-lying unsatisfied urges, the fact is that in the vast majority of cases the offender has been led to find new and more wholesome substitutive satisfactions for his former delinquency, or at least the day has been saved for the healthy development of his personality by alteration of situations which have tended to create his emotional dissatisfactions.

What appears more than anything else to have determined the chance of successful outcome after treatment? In answering this we cannot measure the quality or exact quantity of our effort at treatment since this is so largely a matter of intangibles, subject to the variations inevitably inherent in give-and-take situations where human beings are the prime actors. With all the criticisms that we now, surveying our efforts, could make, we find that there was general adherence to the principle of meeting in each and every case the needs revealed by the study itself. Analyzing our figures on outcomes, the significance of the groupings we have given constantly comes to the fore. If we study the correlations of intelligence levels, of length of time delinquent, of length of time under treatment, of number of times in court or of foster home placement with the outcomes recorded, we find everywhere the cases of Group III showing better results. Of course the figures are not large enough to be statistically satisfying but in the definite trends that are shown they are convincing. The prognosis for the efficacy of treatment at least as far as the family is concerned apparently is clearly related to the grouping. When we find that our treatment apparently resulted in modification of the parents in 67 per cent of the cases in Group III as compared to 24 per cent in Group II, we have no evidence that this was significantly due to higher levels of intelligence in the more modifiable parents, but we do know that their better response was correlated with better life situations and fewer abnormalities among them. It seems, then, that the social pathology which existed in the family circle or outside of it in the cases of Group II so involved the parents or fixed their patterns of living that they were unable or unwilling to face the facts or modify their essential attitudes, behavior tendencies, or conditions of living. Thus it comes out very clearly that with the most skilled treatment that we can offer in our present state of knowledge for the delinquent and for the family the most important determinant of outcome is to be found in our new orientation of prognostic possibilities.

CORRELATION OF INTELLIGENCE LEVELS WITH OUTCOMES

Intelligence quotients		During two or more years following treatment		
		Delinquency ceased	Much improved	Delinquency continued
110 or above	Group I	..	..	4
	Group II	..	1	2
	Group III	5	3	1
90–110	Group I	3	3	7
	Group II	10	3	11
	Group III	29	4	5
80–90	Group I	1	..	3
	Group II	6	3	6
	Group III	13	1	4
72–80	Group I	..	..	1
	Group II	2	..	4
	Group III	..	..	1
66–72	Group I	1	..	1
	Group II	1	..	..
	Group III	..	..	..

(3 unclassified, 1 dead)

AGE OF DELINQUENT WHEN TREATMENT BEGAN CORRELATED WITH OUTCOMES

Groups II and III

Ages	End of treatment period			During two or more years following treatment		
	Delinquency ceased	Much improved	Delinquency continued	Delinquency ceased	Much improved	Delinquency continued
7	1	..	1	1	..	1
8	1	..	2	1	..	2
9	2	..	2	3	1	1
10	5	2	1	6	1	1
11	5	2	3	2	1	9
12	9	3	5	10	3	4
13	11	3	6	7	1	10
14	12	1	6	10	2	6
15	16	2	2	19	..	1
16	4	1	..	2	2	1
17	4	..	3	6	1	..

(1 dead, 1 unknown)

LENGTH OF TIME DELINQUENT BEFORE TREATMENT BEGAN CORRELATED WITH OUTCOMES

Outcome during two or more years following treatment

Length of time delinquent	Group II			Group III		
	Delinquency ceased	Improved	Delinquency continued	Delinquency ceased	Improved	Delinquency continued
About one year or less	2	..	2	23	1	3
From one to three years	8	6	15	13	2	6
From four to nine years	9	1	6	12	2	4

(1 dead)   (1 unknown)

LENGTH OF TIME CASE UNDER TREATMENT CORRELATED WITH OUTCOMES DURING TWO OR MORE YEARS SINCE TREATMENT ENDED

Group I: Median length of service, 14 months, range 4 to 33 months.
Group II: Median length of service, 18 months, range 4 to 36 months.
Group III: Median length of service, 11 months, range 2 to 33 months.

	Group I			Group II			Group III		
	6 months or less	7 to 12 months	12 months or more	6 months or less	7 to 12 months	12 months or more	6 months or less	7 to 12 months	12 months or more
Delinquency ceased	..	1	5	4	5	10	12	13	23
Much improved	..	2	1	1	1	5	1	2	3
Delinquency continued	5	3	7	1	3	19	1	4	7
	(2 unclassified)			(1 dead)			(1 unknown)		

COURT APPEARANCES BEFORE TREATMENT

(On account of their abnormalities court appearances of Group I not significant.)

		Once in court	More than once in court	Not in court
Group II	50 cases	18 (36%)	29 (58%)	3 (6%)
Group III	67 cases	29 (43%)	34 (51%)	4 (6%)
		47	63	7

COURT APPEARANCES BEFORE TREATMENT CORRELATED WITH OUTCOMES DURING TWO OR MORE YEARS SINCE TREATMENT ENDED

	Group II			Group III		
	Delq. ceased	Much improved	Delq. continued	Delq. ceased	Much improved	Delq. continued
Not in court	0	2	1	4	0	0
Once in court	7 (41%)	2	8 (47%)	26 (90%)	0	3 (10%)
More than once in court	12 (41%)	3	14 (48%)	18 (55%)	5	10 (30%)
	(1 dead)			(1 unknown)		

FOSTER HOME PLACEMENT CORRELATED WITH OUTCOMES, ETC., DURING TWO OR MORE YEARS SINCE OUR TREATMENT ENDED

Group I 8 placed	Delinquency ceased	2	1 still in foster home 1 returned to altered home conditions
	Much improved	0	
	Delinquency continued	6	4 in institutions 1 on parole 1 still in foster home
Group II 19 placed	Delinquency ceased	8	4 still in foster homes 3 returned to modified parents 1 returned to altered home conditions
	Much improved	5	4 still in foster homes 1 returned to unmodified parents
	Delinquency continued	6	2 still in foster home 4 returned to unmodified parents (2 now in institutions)
Group III 5 placed	Delinquency ceased	4	all returned to modified parents
	Much improved	1	still in foster home
	Delinquency continued	0	

CHAPTER XIV

PRACTICAL IMPLICATIONS OF THE RESEARCH

THE detailed story of our research conducted for the Institute of Human Relations is ended. At least another volume would be required for more complete case studies, but particularly in the chapter on twins, one delinquent and the other non-delinquent, we have sketched a number of significant life histories. It remains for us to recapitulate some of the material and to state some of the practical implications of the research.

What new light has been gained from these years of intimately knowing in their family life three series of delinquents who were, nearly all of them, already serious offenders? Certainly we should at once state that our own thinking and practice, after our long experience in this field, have been greatly influenced by insights acquired through our investigations and through our experimental approach to the treatment of the problems which cases of delinquency present.

First, it becomes evident from our data that there is practical value in a more penetrating interpretation of delinquency as a form of rational behavior just as dependent on definite causations as is any other form of behavior. In human beings there are urges, desires, and drives seeking satisfaction through various modes of self-expression—and delinquency is one mode of self-expression.

But, we may ask, why and when is delinquency utilized as a means of gaining satisfactions? From our present study there is clear evidence that in the lives of delinquents the ever flowing stream of urges and wishes, which in general follow the broader channels of socially acceptable behavior, has met obstructions or frustrations that cause part of the

Practical Implications

stream to be deflected into currents that sooner or later show the characteristics which we term delinquency. We are convinced that it is possible to discover in nearly every case the nature of these obstructions.

It is commonly held that neighborhood conditions, bad associates, poor recreations, etc., are accountable for the production of delinquency. In truth these are destructive influences, but seeking further it appears that at some varying distance upstream in the sequence of delinquent causation there are almost always deeply felt discomforts arising from unsatisfying human relationships. Herein we have found answer to one of our prime questions: why, living under the same environmental conditions, often inimical, is one child non-delinquent and the other delinquent? The latter we almost universally found to be the one who at some stage of his development had been blocked in his needs for satisfying relationships in his family circle. On the other hand the non-delinquent had nearly always been without any such acute frustrations. His relationships with those in his immediate social environment had been much more satisfying.

It is through the lack of satisfying human relationships that feelings of inadequacy, deprivation, or thwarting are created. When these discomforts are powerfully experienced, the driving forces of wishes and desires naturally develop into urges for substitute satisfactions. When the young individual does not then find satisfactions enough in socially acceptable behavior (or does not develop an inhibiting neurosis), he may find an alternative mode of self-expression through seizing upon the idea of delinquency. Thus delinquency really represents a portion of the stream of human activities which has a strong current behind it. Beginning with various types of discontents at frustrations and continued as a drive for substitute satisfactions, the current has turbulently flowed along into the forms of self-expression that ideas of delinquency have suggested.

We have attempted in an earlier chapter to picture the sequence in a diagram showing the development of delinquent behavior. A rational conception of how the delinquent has experienced frustrations and how he has reacted thereto under the influence of environmental suggestions and invitations that may be termed social pressures forms what we have called our first orientation.

What we have been saying about the significance of delinquency as a general phenomenon represents no mere theoretical or academic consideration. To view delinquency merely as an exhibition of vicious, naughty, or irrational behavior is in utter contradistinction to the scientific standpoint that it has as much specific causation and possibility of being understood as any other manifestation of voluntary activity. The latter way of looking at it involves an orientation that must affect the attitudes which are adopted toward the whole problem. One's conception of the significance of delinquency will shape and direct one's effort and procedure. The acceptance of a scientific orientation concerning causality is the best incentive to the attempt to discover the specific causes for delinquency in a particular case.

THROUGH careful analysis of our accumulated data concerning delinquents and their families it became more and more clear that the delinquent behavior had a very specific meaningfulness for the offender himself. It grew obvious that delinquency as a reactive response represented an attempted solution of the individual's problem; it seemed to promise certain satisfactions; it was a way out of the often blindly felt states of dissatisfaction.

That delinquency is the result of an interplay and a sequence of causes even in the individual case is acknowledged by all students of the subject. Since this is true, it seemed to us that comparative studies of delinquents and non-delinquents, whom we have designated "controls," in the same family might make plain the essentials in cause-and-effect relationships. We might discover what more than anything else differentiated the two groups. Our findings have been that physical status and intellectual level do not in general distinguish the delinquent from his non-delinquent sibling, though they may have importance as factors in the individual case. The same is true of social conditions regarded in and of themselves. Both members of the pairs in almost every case lived in the same homes and in the same neighborhoods. No one can doubt that external influences play a large part in producing delinquency, but our task was to discover whether or not they were primary causes, and why one child seized the environmental invitation to delinquency as a vehicle for self-expression and another felt no urge in that direction or was easily able to conquer it.

In studying personalities we found that the delinquents as a group proved to have the worst developmental histories both from the standpoints of health and response to habit training. Then in marked contradistinction to the controls, delinquents were apt to be overrestless and hyperactive, though it must be granted that this manifestation may often be secondary to emotional experiences and attitudes. Also, if one may judge by this series, there is about one chance in four that the seriously delinquent offender has marked personality deviations. The control very rarely showed such peculiarities.

But though in these matters there were significant differences no one finding was so discriminatory between the pairs as the fact that at least 91 per cent of the delinquents gave clear evidence of being or of having been extremely disturbed because of emotion-provoking relationships with others, mainly with others in the family. We could detect the presence of similar inner stresses in not more than 13 per cent of the controls, and even then to a much less degree. The reasons for the escape from delinquency in these instances were clearly discoverable in terms of counterbalancing satisfactions.

The modern conception of the emotional life as the great dynamic force and of emotional experiences as the most significant conditioning factor in the production of behavior tendencies receives full corroboration from our studies. The extent to which tensions in family situations are involved and the intensity of the feeling reactions to them are seen in our case illustrations and in our collected findings concerning strongly sensed rejections, insecurities, inadequacies, jealousies, mental conflicts, or unhappinesses about family disharmonies. It is of little moment whether our list of the subjective feelings induced by thwartings and deprivations is accepted as finality; the important matter is appreciation of the fact that security in affectional relationships and the individual's desire for personal recognition and attention are involved in these emotional tensions.

Perception of the fact that delinquent behavior has meaningfulness for the individual constitutes, then, a second orientation that we conceive to be absolutely essential to better understanding and better treatment of any serious case of delinquency. As we have said, the offender can be found in the vast majority of instances to be in essential particulars unhappy or unsatisfied. In what way is his delinquent behavior a response to his emotional discomforts? In the chapter, "The Meaningfulness of Delinquency for the Individual," we gave illustrative cases and classified the types of reactive responses in terms of attempts to achieve compensatory satisfactions, attempts to bolster up the ego through obtaining status as a delinquent, to obtain revenge, to win self-aggrandizing satisfactions through antisocial hostilities, or as the giving way to instinctual urges felt to be thwarted. The nature of these responses needs to be interpreted in each case, together with the nature of the underlying emotional

Practical Implications

discomforts to which they are reactions—if there is to be any really rational treatment of delinquency.

Contemplating the fundamental causes of the frustrations to which so much of delinquency is a reaction, it becomes self-evident that processes of dealing with the delinquent by admonition, threat, compulsion, or punishment are almost bound frequently to be failures because such treatment is repressive in character rather than reconstructive. Repression of delinquent tendencies is, of course, sometimes possible for the individual, but only too often when the primary causes are not understood and appropriate treatment is not offered for the individual and for those in his social environment who are influencing him, the end result is continuance in delinquency.

Anyone concerned about good citizenship will agree that a judge confronted with the practical issues of the juvenile court should properly endeavor to create respect for the law, and the point is sometimes made that the delinquent cannot be allowed to gain the impression that delinquency pays. But while older offenders may have definitely crystallized beliefs about profitable returns from antisocial conduct, it is very clear that in childhood and earlier youth delinquency certainly is not entered into as a paying proposition in any ordinary sense. Satisfactions most certainly are striven for as the urges and drives of human nature are at work, but delinquency in these earlier years represents mainly a welling up of blindly active responses.

If at this point it seems that we are developing a philosophy of delinquency, it may be said that our concepts are directly built up from the factual data of our present research.

THIS brings us to our third orientation—a formulated outlook on treatment possibilities.

It would appear from the preceding presentation of orientations that the only logical procedure in treatment would be, as in medical practice, first to determine as far as possible the cause of the symptoms, the real etiology in the case. But granted that our first two orientations illuminate our understanding of causes and give entirely new insights, we find ourselves face-to-face with an important question. Can the continuing situations and conditions which give rise to the dissatisfactions that in turn create the reactive responses called delinquency be satisfactorily modified by treatment? Or if such situations are matters of the past can they be counteracted? In general are treatment methods applicable to these etiological factors once the latter are revealed? What promise of success is there if this scientific method of approaching the case is undertaken? Our query resolves itself into two main parts: (a) Is it possible therapeutically to modify the primary causal factors, which as they affect emotional life are mainly in the social and particularly in the family relationships of the individual? (b) Can treatment with equal chance of success be applied to all delinquents irrespective of personality deviations and other individual differences?

We may return to a medical analogy. Let it be supposed that the symptom, fever, is determined to be caused by tuberculosis. Will the physician be equally hopeful of successfully treating all patients alike, irrespective of the conditions under which they live and without taking into account the constitutional or acquired peculiarities of the individual, such as are bound to complicate treatment? As a matter of fact he knows full well that if the patient continues to live in an environment that is defective from the standpoint of hygiene or even that is productive of unhealthy mental states the outlook is poor. Also he has to diagnose and allow for other than tubercular pathological conditions in the individual. These may require long-time experimental treatment with observation of the patient's reactions thereto, perhaps prolonged segregation in special institutions. Thus life situations and the patients themselves present great dissimilarities that are important for consideration in the therapeutic endeavor.

Just so with delinquents. In spite of the fiction of the law that all men are equal before it, offenders represent many diverse kinds of human material, and the life experiences and situations which directly produce delinquent trends vary greatly. Taking the general factors that we found in the vast majority of cases, a scheduled analogy to cases of tuberculosis may be as follows:

	The Patient	*The Delinquent*
Symptom:	Fever	Delinquency
Diagnosis:	Reaction of organism attempting to combat tubercular infection	Reaction of individual attempting to obtain compensating satisfactions
Etiology: (cause)	Special pathology of tuberculosis	Special emotional discomforts caused by unsatisfying human relationships
Considerations for prognosis and treatment program:	Physical characteristics of patient—constitutional or the result of other disease	Personality characteristics of delinquent—constitutional or the result of any earlier experiences
	Living conditions and their possible modification	Social and particularly family relationships and their possible modification
	Extent or stage of the disease	Extent of delinquent ideation and its hold upon the individual

We can see at once that treatment for delinquency applied as if offenders form a homogeneous group leads to a tremendous amount of wasted effort. For the sake of economies of various kinds there can be vastly better estimation of what is accomplishable and vastly better planning. Though we may discern that fundamental causes almost always relate to the emotional disturbances that we have outlined, it is quickly found in practice that the same treatment of these causes is not universally applicable and that the prognosis is not equally good for every case.

Before tracing the outcomes in our series of cases, we found that for a diagnostic and prognostic classification three major groups were distinguishable. Moreover this grouping was undertaken at the most strategic point in our research, namely, after the treatment period was ended. Hence, no preconceptions of what therapy would or would not be availing directed in any way the amount or kind of therapeutic endeavor. As we said earlier, in order that our research should properly represent an experimental approach to all the problems that delinquency presents, our efforts were exerted without any prejudgment of what might or might not prove successful. Indeed many of the most difficult personalities and unpromising family situations received the most attention.

These groupings represent a first blocking out of a prognostic framework for considering treatment possibilities. Through more research, subdivisions of these groupings may later be found to be advisable but the validity of our major groupings seems clearly evidenced by the recorded outcomes following our treatment period.[1]

	Group I	Group II	Group III
		Percentages	
Definitely non-delinquent during follow-up period	19	38	72
Delinquency definitely continued	58	46	19

Not reiterating our discussion of Group I in Chapter XI, suffice it here to say that for highly practical purposes there

1. For complete figures on outcomes, etc., see Chapter XI.

should be considered in one group those delinquents whose personality deviations and abnormalities or whose neurotic conflicts lead them to be so unstable, so weak in inhibitory powers that the prognosis for checking their delinquent trends without highly specialized and long continued treatment is very poor.[2] Even though we ascertain that they have felt thwarted or deprived or have developed deep feelings of inadequacy there are so many other complications in the characteristics of the individuals themselves that treatment merely directed to their emotional discomforts without their being placed in a controlled environment is almost certain to be unavailing.

Cases of this group present medicopsychological, social, and re-educative problems. What can be done with and for them can only be determined by well-directed research conducted during prolonged segregation. If such a proposal seems costly, one can answer that many such delinquents develop careers of crime that are vastly more expensive than long continued programs of treatment would be. As it is, they sooner or later receive sentences that involve years of incarceration, usually without benefit to the offender and with no knowledge accruing of how better to treat others of the same type when young. And then it must be remembered that because of their lack of inhibitions and their aggressiveness cases of these types are great sources of delinquent contagion, often stimulating others to be offenders. Our studies of earlier years contain many instances of this sort. It is an important finding in the present study that the varied and in many cases intensive treatment efforts on our part yielded such slight accomplishment with these cases.

Certainly the diagnosis in most instances can only be made through expert study, but teachers, juvenile court judges,

2. Though excluded from this study because the welfare of society so obviously demands their prolonged or even permanent custodial care, mental defectives showing personality deviations with established delinquent trends should, of course, also be included in Group I.

probation officers, and institution officials trained to be aware of possible clues could have such studies made. For developing treatment possibilities which, as we have indicated, must largely be upon an experimental and research basis, new resources of a hospital type and a professional personnel are needed. This most certainly will require new legislation in order that funds may be provided and long time segregation be made possible.

GROUP II consists of cases where the delinquent is confronted by unwholesome situations within or outside the family circle that seem only with great difficulty, if at all, alterable. For their remedy radical measures would be required, such as are ordinarily quite beyond the powers of those dealing with delinquents. Knowledge of the fact that these conditions have been provocative of the emotional disturbances lying at the roots of the delinquent's behavior does not help much to nullify the influences deriving from the social pathology. These are so actively potent in the delinquent's life that little headway can be made in his treatment if he remains in his old environment; the situation pulls down faster than efforts at reconstructive treatment can build up. Simple or more complex, for they usually are multiple, the unfortunate conditions weigh heavily against successful treatment of the etiological factors which lie back of the symptomatic manifestation, delinquency. Any conception that the delinquent can be immunized against such situations is rarely well founded, at least until he can gain the emotional and perhaps economic independence that naturally is not a possibility for him in younger years.

A long list could, of course, be given of the obstructive social situations that are the barriers to satisfying relationships or to finding socially acceptable substitutive satisfactions. We have shown something of the social pathology, ranging from family life with mentally abnormal, alcoholic, unscrupulous, hating, or thoroughly indifferent parents to inadequate income, crowded housing, and neighborhood conditions with much incitement to delinquency. In very few cases which we placed in Group II were there families that demonstrated normally good standards of living and behavior; in these instances the social pathology was mainly in delinquent companionship.

It is true that there were non-delinquents in all these families, but as we discovered by our studies of the controls this was commonly due to the fact that, unlike the delinquents, they had some definitely satisfying relationship to a parent or to a parent surrogate, sometimes even to a parent of poor type. Or in the few cases where we found the non-delinquents to have some degree of emotional disturbance about their relationships to others they were able to find counterbalancing satisfactions in other affectional ties or in special achievements.

It is obvious that there must be great waste of effort in attempting to check delinquency by dealing alone with the delinquent who continues to live under such circumstances. But, though we made an earnest approach to each of the 50 families of Group II in an endeavor to give understanding of the delinquent's needs and to cultivate parental responsibilities, we found many attitudes and conditions unmodifiable by any means at our command. It was only to be expected that practically all of the delinquents who remained at home in such situations, in general against our advice, had poor records during the follow-up period.[3]

By dint of much effort, we did find in a minority of the cases that some of the deeper causal relationships were modifiable, though it is too much to expect that even such mea-

3. The details of outcomes correlated with treatment are given in Chapter XII.

gerly good results would obtain in similar cases without the great amount of work that was made possible by our research equipment.

Placing in good foster homes while re-educative contacts were maintained both with the delinquent and his family showed the best results, but any return of a former delinquent to unchanged family relationships and to bad neighborhood conditions nearly always meant renewed delinquency. Our long prior experience has shown that mere placing away from home for a period does not immunize the child against recurrence of old or development of new dissatisfactions or incitements to delinquency. Not infrequently the need for the delinquent is to remain in a good foster home for a very long time, and with the parents' full coöperation, for the child's emotional pull toward his own home is often very great, though it be a poor home. The work of even the best child-placing agencies proves ineffectual in the long run unless these conditions are met. One of the difficulties arises through the belief of some juvenile court judges in the efficacy of short-time placing. Their attitude often is that if a child has done well he has the *right* to return home. Or perhaps the judge makes the finding that the parents have *their rights* to the child if they demand his return. Taking such a stand always seems to us much as if, when a patient shows the capacity to recover from an illness under an improved life situation, he should be allowed to go back to the conditions which originally gave him the disease.

We ourselves see the possibility that long-time placing may create immunity, but only with the growth into maturity and into the emotional independence that we have al-

4. Some years ago we made a special study, *Reconstructing Behavior in Youth,* 1929, of the immediate results of selective foster-home placing and found them remarkably good, proving that in the vast majority of cases where the delinquent did not show personality deviations it was very possible to check delinquent tendencies. But we have followed the cases then studied after an interval of years and discover that upon return to inimical conditions a majority sooner or later reverted to delinquency.

Practical Implications 213

ready mentioned. Expensive this may be but, again, not so costly as criminal careers.

With regard to institutional treatment, a good deal of what we have said about the return to an unfit environment is just as applicable.[5] However, being held long in a correctional school for maturity to develop is apt to be a great detriment to the individual—the institution is an artificial environment that does not prepare for community life. The well-known stigma of "the reform school" is a handicap even though only subjectively as when a sense of inferiority is engendered through having been an "inmate."

What, then, is the greatest hope for prevention or cure of delinquency in the type of cases that belong in Group II? There can be little doubt that improvement of general social conditions, economic, housing, recreational (80 per cent of these cases come from areas of high rates of delinquency) would cause the group to shrink in size. But we have to remember that the deeper essential causes are to be found in the special relationships of the delinquent with those in his immediate environment. Is there any hope that parents can be convinced strongly enough or held strongly enough by court procedure so that they will amend their essential attitudes and behavior? Or can they be helped through any source to solve their own problems and to change their feelings, attitudes and behavior?

Certainly something could be accomplished, but considering the ignorances, the set of life habits, and the circumstances of most of these parents it would require a carefully conducted demonstration to show that, and how, courts could to any extent overcome such inimical conditions. Nevertheless until for its own protection society does assume in some way

---

5. A recent Children's Bureau (U.S. Dept. of Labor) publication, No. 230, gives the result of tracing the after-careers of 621 boys who were in five of the best known correctional institutions. It was found that 66 per cent had been arrested and 58 per cent convicted one or more times after having been paroled from the institution.

social control over its members whose behavior is a great factor in producing delinquency in their children, society will have to continue to pay the high cost of delinquency and crime.

The larger programs of special and coöperative effort at prevention of delinquency we leave for discussion a little later.

GROUP III is a diagnostic and prognostic classification made through the process of elimination—it contains all those who are not markedly neurotic or personality deviates and those whose life situations do not present the gross social pathology we have just been discussing. The delinquents may have and frequently have had just as long careers. Fortunately, even among our serious offenders, Group III forms the largest group.

That these delinquents, equally with those in the other groups, had deep emotional disturbances arising from faulty family relationships should go without saying in the light of our general findings. Nor had they shown, more than the others, any tendency to self-initiated cessation of delinquency. For them and their families expert aid was needed for the cultivation of better insights and for re-education in attitudes. The amount of psychiatric and other treatment given, however, was no more, indeed it averaged somewhat less in length, than was attempted for cases in the other groups. That the response of parents was greater we should naturally expect from the fact that the social pathology was less extreme, with all that this connotes.

As might have been anticipated, the favorable results were vastly greater than for either of the other groups. During the follow-up period 72 per cent remained non-delinquent, while 19 per cent definitely continued in delinquency. The causes for even this percentage of failures we have earlier analyzed.

THE validity of this new orientation concerning prognosis and treatment once more becomes evident. If we were beginning a new research, building on our present conclusions, we should feel warranted in making very little therapeutic effort with cases belonging to Group I after careful observation had convinced us of the diagnosis—unless treatment were instituted under the conditions of experimental research that we have before mentioned. Truth to tell, nobody at the present time knows how to treat such cases successfully.

Under present social conditions we advocate for Group II the development of adequate resources for good foster-home treatment with the possibility of long-time care. Treatment with the delinquent and the foster family should be continued, facing all the needs as they exist or may arise. At the same time strong effort at re-educative treatment should be made with all families that seem really responsive, since their modification might mean the possibility of earlier return of delinquents. An incidental though important by-product would be the prevention of delinquency among the other children.

From the standpoint of potential success we consider Group III as warranting the major therapeutic endeavor. Our research shows that many families among these where the social pathology is not excessive can be re-educated to establish new relationships with their children. If this was the experience of our clinics, we should conceive it to be an extremely practical point for all who are attempting to deal reconstructively with delinquents.

Though of course we recognized emotional stresses and in every case made at least some attempt to meet them, we did not know initially that they would constitute the outstanding feature differentiating delinquents and non-delinquents. Had we been aware of this, we would have watched even more carefully to see to what degree various treatment measures met the delinquent's emotional problems. It is now our belief that such centering of our concern would have made some differences in our treatment procedures and would possibly have led to some better outcomes, particularly in Group III cases.

ALTOGETHER it can be seen that our research into fundamental causes has left us with the conviction that the checking of a delinquent career once started is no easy matter. In any treatment project there is no royal road to success. And, we are afraid, the same must be said about prevention in general. For the sake of relief from our extraordinary national burden of delinquency and crime, much greater interest must be manifested not only in expert work with individual offenders, but also in mass attacks upon the whole problem.

Within the last few years there have been an increasing number of programs of this latter kind. They are all to be welcomed, though none of them have been existent long enough to be competently evaluated. As in our own study, a follow-up period in which critically to scrutinize results with scientific objectivity is an essential to knowledge of the value of any project. And this is true whether the project take the form of recreational activities in clubs or settlements, occupational training in camps, control through so-called coördinating councils, or any of the various schemes organized in school systems. It may well be that some considerable number of offenders can through such mass efforts find substitutive satisfactions and new points of view that will supplant their previous delinquent tendencies—certainly that is the hope and aim of such programs. But we are frank to wonder whether with the seriously delinquent, when such underlying factors as we have discovered remain untouched, the individual will continue to be non-delinquent after he is without these aids to better living. Once the props are with-

Practical Implications 217

drawn, at what age or under what circumstances can the former delinquent be expected to "make good"?

As a logical outgrowth of our study which shows that parent-child relationships play such a huge part in the production of delinquent proclivities we are inclined to believe that the single direct attack of greatest value may be through widespread parental education—to be sure not an easy task. However, national and local organizations are taking steps in this direction. Not that the mere reading of newspaper columns or periodicals on child care, or attendance at a course of lectures will suffice. Parents must gain insights into the fact that their own emotional attitudes, so often unconsciously motivated, as well as the feeling life of their children are involved in any behavior problems presented. Is it too much to hope that there might be neighborhood councils even in poorer districts, with group meetings of parents where under psychiatrically trained leadership individual and community problems could openly be discussed? Under many conditions it is hardly possible for families to prevent delinquency among their children without such community coöperations, though parents gain more insights and have the best of intentions. Only greater public awareness of the value of parental education plus social coöperation can bring about the more general establishment of both.

When early signs of delinquency are detected, parents, unless they find themselves immediately able to cope with the problem, should be educated to act as they should in a case of impending serious illness, namely, voluntarily to seek and carry out the recommendations of professional service in a clinic where behavior difficulties are studied and expertly treated. The relatively good outcomes in cases where families were willing to take such attitudes is amply shown in the present research. A difficulty arises when court authorities attempt to force clinical consultations without persuasively educating parents concerning the part that they should and could play in uncovering the facts of causation and in remedying them.

And then how to combat certain unfortunate parts of our national ideology! It is certainly partly on account of widespread sets of ideas about it that our children so readily utilize delinquency as a means of self-expression when they have dissatisfactions. The conception of delinquency as a possible and even an attractive mode of behavior looms large in the American scene. There is very much less of this in other countries where children, too, must have thwartings and dissatisfactions.

Kinberg, the Swedish psychiatrist and criminologist, knowing America and looking at us from the European viewpoint observes our unique scale of social values.[6] We as a new country have not, he says, the advantage of a heritage of moral standards. Our heterogeneous population presents a great variety of moral conceptions which are mobile, owing to the intensity of our own social processes of disorganization and reorganization. "American society is still largely in a seething, eruptive and highly dramatic state." The display of great wealth and the knowledge of the ease with which it often has been accumulated offer seductive examples to our people. Laws that we pass have slight influence on public opinion or morals; personal behavior patterns are modeled much more by the attitudes of immediate associates. And this last accounts, thinks Kinberg, for "the openly criminal methods frequently met with in American administration and policy." (He evidently means our prevalent political and business attitudes and competitive unfairnesses.) Then among us we have general recognition of the fact that crime is lucrative. Nowhere else does it offer anything like the same returns.

In considering the ways through which ideas of crime are

6. Olof Kinberg, *Basic Problems of Criminology*, Copenhagen, 1935.

communicated, Kinberg dwells on the tremendous extent to which crime news is published in America. He approvingly quotes W. I. Thomas: "A people is profoundly influenced by what is persistently brought to its attention." Skillful advertising is, of course, based on this psychological fact. If that public institution, the press, makes the citizenry continually acquainted with the frequency and successes of criminal exploits, it to a considerable degree lessens the feeling against crime and so lowers the barriers to it. And Kinberg feels that quite apart from any results of picturing crime, the movies by glorifying wealth irrespective of the way in which it is acquired have a similar effect.

We may do well to contemplate what this philosophic observer has to say about us, but any competent student of delinquency could add other relevant points concerning the life of our young people. General and specific social and economic conditions; our machine-made modes of living so that the modern child has few educative responsibilities in the home or in apprentice employment; through growth of urban life the lack of outlets for adventure-loving youth; the tempting chances for delinquency that the omnipresent automobile in various ways affords; local or group antisocial sets of ideas; all these and many other matters are involved.

With the whole picture in mind, we can leave to our imagination what some new awakening spirit of good citizenship might bring about. Just for the sake of our national or local pride, to say nothing of the flowering of our civilization, what would it mean to have a general spirit of right social living in which delinquency would be generally condemned by young people themselves. No business-like war on crime by the Department of Justice "G-men," a war that we find provokes youthful admiration for bravery on either side, and no mere repressive measures for combatting delinquency can possibly accomplish what a better type of general feeling for the values of socialized living might produce.

A reformative program for the defects in our national methods of living and in our ideologies would demand the acquirement of whole sets of new social values and of new personal standards and conceptions of responsibilities on the part of many of our citizens and particularly of our leaders in public life and in business—they who, whether they realize it or not, are definitely influencing the ideas and secondarily the behavior of our people, even of our children. With all the vast modern exhibition of growth in power to understand and utilize the forces of the material world and with all the progress that has been possible in the biological sciences, including the control of physical disease, must we merely wait, as our European friends suggest, for a better tradition of social behavior slowly to evolve—perhaps in another hundred or five hundred years!

While the present research has augmented our prior knowledge of what is going on in this day and generation that tends continuously to produce delinquency, our task has been to accept the American scene as it is and work with delinquents and their families in the midst of many conditions which we regard as unfortunate. If it remains for us to discuss at all publicly administered or other organized projects for combatting delinquency, we can only do so with an eye to their weaknesses and betterment. An entirely new research and probably a very valuable one could center on what can be discovered that is administratively producing really good results with any large percentages of already or potentially seriously delinquent offenders.

What we do see very plainly is that at present there is very little general conception of the possibilities of getting away from largely worthless and non-curative methods of dealing with cases of serious delinquency. It might almost be said that we are still in the dark ages, or at least in the pre-scientific era of treatment of juvenile delinquents. And one main reason for this surely is the fact brought out by the present research, namely that the causes for delinquency, some of them superficially discernible in easily observed conditions, are really complex. Well-oriented treatment procedures need the facts that can be obtained only by scientifically directed explorations of, to use our earlier simile, the upstream sources of the current that flows in the channels of delinquency.

Now the training for making such explorations or even for appreciating the value and the practical implications of them is certainly not derived through a legal education. To be sure, for long there has been a cry for specially trained judges in juvenile courts, but the supply of them is very meager—and so what is to be expected! And this is only one matter for consideration because the actual treatment of juvenile offenders lies much more in the hands of probation officers, institutional authorities and parole officers. What proportion of these are trained enough or are intelligent enough to get at and break down the obstructions to socially acceptable behavior which exist so frequently in human relationships and affect the mental and particularly the emotional life of the child? With all that is at stake in the treatment of young human beings there are ordinarily less training requirements for those who are expected to alter the conduct tendencies of delinquents than there are for those who treat sick cattle.

It is not infrequently argued nowadays that the juvenile court has proven itself not to be an effective agency for the checking of delinquency and the prevention of criminal careers.[7] But, frankly, do we yet know under what other organized scheme there could be a better initial approach to

7. For perhaps the best short statement of the difficulties with juvenile courts—one that has come to hand since the above was written—see "The Juvenile Courts," by Grace Abbott, formerly head of the Federal Children's Bureau, *The Survey,* May, 1936. Herein it is definitely suggested that some other social service agencies should be developed to undertake treatment of juvenile delinquents.

treatment of the problems presented by a case of serious delinquency? As we have said above, a number of other preventive and reformative projects are afoot with admirable programs, but they are all as yet on trial so far as possible accomplishment with definitely delinquent youth is concerned. With serious cases authority under the law is undoubtedly a necessity and thus whatever its designation the agency handling them will be *de facto* a juvenile court.

Even through our present studies of a relatively small number of delinquents and their families we have ample evidences of the possible untoward effects of some juvenile court procedures. Again we have noted the hardening effect of detention home incarcerations—the natural results of throwing delinquents together without constructive understandings and adjustments of their difficulties, with no segregation of the unsophisticated from the worst teachers of vice and youthful criminality, and with nearly all of the delinquents in that anxious and suggestible state of mind that precedes adjudication of their case in court. Then we have witnessed the arousal of uncoöperative and resistive attitudes on the part of offenders and of parents as the result of anger displayed by a judge or because of threats made in court. On the other hand kindly leniency also offered without understanding leads some offenders to see the court as a symbol of social weakness. The strong hand or an attitude of forbearance without the scientific approach may be equally ineffective.

There are many features of the machinery of the juvenile court and of the attitudes taken in it and created by it which may well challenge the personnel of a court to attempt betterment.

The juvenile court is recognized as a great American institution; much credit has been given to this country for its establishment. In consequence it is not easily to be uprooted and have its functions transferred. It goes without saying that apart from their other functions juvenile courts do exert helpful influences with many delinquents and their families; the problem is how they are progressively to institute scientifically guided programs of treatment for delinquency. Any popular clamor against handling delinquents by soft methods should find nothing to criticize in the scientific attitude and in the backing for it that a juvenile court should offer. If a judge appeals to a family in some such terms as, "There must be something that has been going wrong in your family life or in the delinquent's relationships that has to be understood and altered," he is taking anything but a weak stand in the case. An attempt to gain scientific understanding is never softness.

We are still constrained to believe in the administrative possibilities of a commission or tribunal composed of experts from several fields who should have complete charge of all treatment of cases of serious delinquency after adjudication of the fact. Such a commission must necessarily give full time service and have state-wide authority. We see no other way in which treatment can be consistently and consecutively administered, utilizing all possible public and private resources for treatment and planning new ones. Apparently no other scheme or organization can induce satisfactory coöperation between juvenile courts, expert clinical service, private and public social agencies, schools, correctional institutions, and parole officers. In the light of what we have been able to show, such coöperation is absolutely essential and is lacking at present.

In a final word and without attempting to suggest any final solution to the administrative problems which we know are difficult but should not be insurmountable, we insist with the greatest assurance that any and all methods of administering treatment for the seriously delinquent will fail unless certain fundamental conceptions that have been outlined as the result of this research are utilized. The practical implications of our findings are that little can be accomplished under any organization or programs for treatment unless there is recognition of the significance of our new orientations and the development of a personnel to put these principles into practice.

INDEX

Abbott, G., 221
Adjustments, emotional, 48–50, 52
Age, of delinquents, 37, 50, 190–191, 197; vs. controls, 55–56, 73
Alcoholism, 28, 38
Alexander, F., 184
Ascendance, *see* Submission

Bronner, A. F., 162

Case studies, of emotional experience, 123; of contrasting emotional experiences, 124–125, 125–126, 126–128; in favorable family, 81–83; of Group I, 176–177; of Group II, 181; of Group III, 184–188; on meaningfulness of delinquency, 137–138, 138–139, 139–140; of twins, 95–97, 98–100, 100–102, 102–106, 107–110, 110–112, 112–115, 116–119
Childers, A. T., 45
Cinema, 72, 135
Clubs, 71–72
Compensation, 112, 120, 130, 133 f., 195, 204
Conceptions, ethical, 46, 66–67
Conscience, *see* Superego
Controls, 54 ff.: vs. delinquents, age, 55–56; school attitudes, 62; personality characteristics, 62–73; personality deviations, 58–59; in favorable families, 78–85, 89–91; in inimical families, 85–89; physical habits, 59–60; intelligence, 60–61; personalities, 53–55; scholarship, 61–62; sex, 56; physical status, 56
Courts, Juvenile, 146–147, 148, 205, 221–222

Defectives, mental, 17, 162–163; physical, 3, 39–43, 51–52, 56–57, 87, 163; delinquents vs. controls, 73–74

Deviations, physical, *see* Defectives, physical
Disease, *see* Defectives, physical
Dissatisfaction, *see* Frustration
Disturbances, emotional, *see* Frustration

Ego, satisfaction of, 5, 6, 9, 98, 100, 102, 106, 110, 134
Emotions, display of, 45–46, 52, 77; experienced by delinquents vs. controls, 121–131; types of disturbances, 128–129
Endocrines, disturbances of, 3, 40–41, 74, 79, 89
Enuresis, 59–60, 74
Environment, 50
Epilepsy, *see* Personality, epileptic
Extroversion, *see* Introversion

Family, 1 f., 9 f., 12–13, 13, 16, 23, 25–35, 47–48, 53 ff., 121, 141 ff., 158 ff., 202 f.; attitude of, toward delinquency, 31–32; education of, 28; ethical standards of, 28; favorable, 78–85, 89–91; income of, 27; inimical, 85–89; intelligence of, 28; nationality of, 27, 34; personalities in, 28; position in, 50; religion of, 27, 30–31, 34; social condition of, 29, 34–35; treatment of, 146–153, 154–157, 175, 180, 182, 217–218
Fantasy life, 47, 67–70
Frustration, 7, 45, 48, 97–98, 100, 102, 106, 110, 112, 115, 128–129, 132–133, 162, 200 ff.

Glueck, E. T., 158
Glueck, S., 158
Gregariousness, 63–64

Habits, 47, 52; physical, of delinquents vs. controls, 59–60, 75
Haldane, J. B. S., 93

Health, *see* Defectives, physical
Healy, W., 39, 184
Heredity, 38, 39
History, developmental, of delinquents vs. controls, 56–57, 74
Hobbies, 72–73
Homes, broken, 27, 35; foster, 37, 193–194, 199, 212, 215
Homosexuality, 42, 75, 102–110, 163

Ideas, source of, 68–70, 135–136, 218–219
Identification, 10
Illegitimacy, 27, 35, 50, 73
Inferiority, feeling of, 46–47, 49, 65–66, 90, 119–120, 130
Inhibition, forces of, 10, 58, 88–89, 209
Intelligence, 18, 41, 52, 190, 196; delinquents vs. controls, 60–61, 75–76, 203; and treatment, 190, 196
Interests, 47, 52, 87; of delinquents vs. controls, 70–71, 77
Introversion, 47, 52, 58, 65, 87
Israelite, J., 163

Kinberg, O., 218

Lange, J., 93

Masturbation, 52, 75
Methodology, 14–24, 36, 142–145, 158–159

Needs, *see* Wishes
Neurosis, 42–43, 58, 75, 89, 161 ff., 173–174, 209

Parents, *see* Family
Personality, characteristics of, 44–47, 52; characteristics of delinquents vs. controls, 62–73, 203; delinquents vs. controls, 58–59, 75–77; epileptic, 38–39, 42, 74
Prognosis, 160–172, 207
Prostitution, 38
Psychosis, 38, 39, 42–43, 58, 75, 89, 163, 173
Psychotherapy, *see* Treatment

Reading, 52, 72, 135

Recidivism, 37, 51, 163–164, 192, 198
Reform, *see* Remedies
Relationships, social, 48–50, 52, 90
Religion, 70–71, 77
Remedies, for delinquency, 210, 213–214, 215, 216–224
Repression, 195, 205
Restlessness, 44–45, 62–63, 94

Scholarship, 48; delinquents vs. controls, 61–62, 76
School, attitudes toward, of delinquents vs. controls, 62
Selfishness, 47
Sex, of delinquents, 50; delinquents vs. controls, 56, 73
Shaw, C., 86
Shimberg, M. E., 163
Social workers, 18, 30, 143 ff., 150
Spaulding, E. R., 39
Sports, 72
Step-parents, 27, 35, 73
Submission, 52, 64–65
Sunday school, 70–71
Superego, 12
Sutherland, E. H., 162

Therapy, *see* Treatment
Thomas, W. I., 219
Treatment, of delinquents, 2, 16, 18 f., 30, 41, 143, 143–145, 153–154, 158–172, 173–189, 205 ff.; educational, 149; institutional, 213; physical, 18 f., 143; psychiatric, 18 f., 30, 143, 150; results of, 164–165, 168–169, 170–171, 172, 176, 178–179, 181–182, 182, 195–196, 208, 211–212, 214; social, 149–150
Truancy, 3, 6, 136
Twins, 24, 92–120; identical, 93
Types of delinquency, 37–38, 51

Urges, *see* Needs

Values, social, 218–219; subjective, 133 ff.

Wishes, 2 ff., 23, 25 f., 94, 132 f., 162, 200

Young, K., 162